# Business Writing Made Simple

## A Manager's Handbook

Stephen D. Bruce, Ph.D., *Editor in Chief*

**BLR**

**BUSINESS & LEGAL REPORTS**

BUREAU OF LAW & BUSINESS, INC. • HAZARDOUS WASTE BULLETIN

64 WALL STREET, MADISON, CT 06443-1513

**Editorial Staff:**

Editor in Chief: Stephen D. Bruce, Ph.D.

Managing Editor: Frank R. Abate
Editorial Associates: Gillian M. Akel, Regina Robert
Editorial Assistants: Mary Backer, Jo-Ann P. Milici
Art Director: John F. Kallio

---

© 1986 BUSINESS & LEGAL REPORTS

First Printing

All rights reserved. This book may not be reproduced in part or in whole by any process without written permission from the publisher.

ISBN 1-55645-421-X

Printed in the United States of America

# Table of Contents

## SECTION I: Guidelines for Effective Business Writing
1. The Basics of Better Business Writing ................................................. 1
2. How to Write — The Five-step System ................................................. 7

## SECTION II: Sample Letters and Memos
3. Recruitment ........................................................................................ 27
4. Employment Issues ............................................................................ 37
5. Motivation .......................................................................................... 47
6. Personal Touches ............................................................................... 51
7. Administration ................................................................................... 61

## SECTION III: Writing Effective Management Reports
8. Five Steps to Writing Effective Reports ............................................. 75
9. Special Management Reports ............................................................ 99

## SECTION IV: Writers' Appendices
I. Trite Word/Phrase Replacements ..................................................... 109
II. Punctuation Rules ............................................................................. 111
III. Formal Forms of Address ................................................................. 119
IV. Footnotes and Bibliographies ........................................................... 125
V. Using Tables and Graphs in Reports ................................................. 131
VI. Similar Words ................................................................................... 137
VII. Colloquial Expressions ..................................................................... 161
VIII. Latin Words and Phrases .................................................................. 165
IX. Superfluous Words ........................................................................... 169
X. The Right Preposition ....................................................................... 173
XI. Commonly Misspelled Words ........................................................... 179

# Table of Samples

## SECTION I

### Chapter 2. How to Write—The Five-Step System
Formal Style Letter .................................................................................................. 12
Semiformal Style Letter ........................................................................................... 13
Familiar Style Letter ................................................................................................ 14
Memo ....................................................................................................................... 15
Outline ..................................................................................................................... 16
Informal Outline ...................................................................................................... 17

## SECTION II

### Chapter 3. Recruitment
Advertising for Job Openings
    Display Ads ...................................................................................................... 27
    Classified Ads ................................................................................................... 29
Setting Up Applicant Interviews .............................................................................. 30
Declining an Interview ............................................................................................. 31
Accepting an Applicant ............................................................................................ 32
Turning Down an Applicant .................................................................................... 33
Welcome to New Employee ..................................................................................... 34
Orientation ............................................................................................................... 35

### Chapter 4. Employment Issues
Recommendations/References .................................................................................. 37
Verification of Employment ..................................................................................... 40
Credit References ..................................................................................................... 41
Personnel Evaluations
    Evaluation Checklist for Clerical Positions .................................................... 43
    Evaluation Checklist for Managerial Positions ............................................... 44
    Writing Skills Guidelines ................................................................................. 46

### Chapter 5. Motivation
Special Recognition
    For Civic Service .............................................................................................. 47
    For Professional Honor .................................................................................... 48
    To an Employee for a Job Well Done ............................................................. 48
Goodwill
    To Employees at Year End .............................................................................. 49
    To Customer, Newly Promoted ....................................................................... 49

### Chapter 6. Personal Touches
Announcements
    Birth of First Child .......................................................................................... 51
    Birth of Subsequent Children .......................................................................... 51
    Adoption ........................................................................................................... 52
Announcement of Retirement
    To Employee .................................................................................................... 52
    To Company .................................................................................................... 53

|                                                         |    |
|---------------------------------------------------------|----|
| To Customers                                            | 53 |
| Invitations, Formal                                     |    |
|     Issuing                         | 55 |
|     Accepting                       | 56 |
|     Declining                       | 56 |
| Invitations, Informal                                   |    |
|     Issuing                         | 57 |
|     Accepting                       | 57 |
|     Declining                       | 57 |
| Invitations, Letterhead                                 | 58 |
| Condolences                                             |    |
|     To Business Associate of the Deceased | 59 |
|     To a Widow(er) of an Employee   | 59 |
|     Upon Personal Injury or Illness | 59 |
| Fund Raising                                            | 60 |

## Chapter 7. Administration

| | |
|---|---|
| Acknowledging Letters Received in Co-worker's Absence | 61 |
| Confirmations | 63 |
| Authorizations | 64 |
| Initiating Work | 65 |
| Letters of Transmittal | 66 |
| Requesting Information | 67 |
| Requesting Reservations | 68 |
| Requesting a Speaker | 69 |
| Minutes | 70 |

# SECTION III

## Chapter 8. Five Steps to Effective Reports

| | |
|---|---|
| Report Outline | 83 |
| Type I Report | 91 |

## Chapter 9. Special Management Reports

| | |
|---|---|
| Departmental Status Report | 100 |
| Progress Report | 101 |
| Research Report Summary | 102 |
| Management Recommendation | 105 |

# Section I
# Guidelines for Effective Business Writing

# Chapter 1

# The Basics of Better Business Writing

Writing is the key to effective business communication. You know how important it is to success. Writing is essential for everyday communication, and *good* writing puts power behind your ideas. But sometimes the task seems insurmountable—you don't know where to begin. And once you start, you may be unsure about how you should proceed and when to end. What's more, you know you will be evaluated by how effectively you handle these writing tasks. All this is enough to make anyone nervous.

Now you can relax because you are about to learn the secrets that experienced, professional business writers use whenever they sit down to write. You'll learn how they approach the writing task, and how they successfully complete it. By following the simple guidelines contained in this volume, you, too, will soon be producing effective, professional correspondence and reports. Writing you will be proud of, and that will make others proud of you, is within your reach.

## HOW THIS BOOK WILL HELP

This book will provide you with a practical guide that you can use every day to make sure your writing is getting your point across—no matter what the point is and no matter to whom you're writing. It covers the basics of effective writing to ensure that you are conveying the message that you intend. It presents samples of all the kinds of writing that you use most often. Plus, the appendices provide a convenient reference source to refer to whenever you are in doubt about just the right word.

The book has four sections:

**Section I: Guidelines for Effective Business Writing**

Learn how to make anything you write come out clearly and convincingly by following the guidelines outlined in the first section. Learn how to plan and present your ideas in the most effective way.

**Section II: Sample Letters and Memos**

Use the Table of Samples in the front of this book to select a sample letter, memo or report that most closely matches your own project. Use it as a model. Many samples are preceded by a checklist of items that should be included. Use this checklist to make sure you have included everything before you send your letter or memo. By using these samples as models and following the guidelines in Section I, you'll be able to get what you want by using the right words in the right form.

**Section III: Writing Effective Management Reports**

Report writing requires special techniques which are outlined in detail. This chapter takes you through the process of this most important kind of writing. When you follow the step-by-step guidelines, you can be assured that the results of your work will be presented in a complete, clear, organized manner.

**Section IV: Writers' Appendices**

The eleven comprehensive writers' appendices help you make sure you are using the appropriate words and form to ensure successful results. Appendices include:

- Trite Words/Phrase Replacements
- Punctuation Rules
- Forms of Address
- Footnotes and Bibliographies
- Tables and Graphs in Reports
- Similar Words
- Colloquial Expressions
- Latin Words and Phrases
- Superfluous Words
- The Right Preposition
- Commonly Misspelled Words

Think of the book as a guide and research tool for all your writing. Keep it on your desk to refer to each time you need to write. Use Section I to plan, organize, and word your document, then select a sample from Section II or III that closely resembles your project and just follow the format presented there. If necessary, use Section IV to answer special questions on wording or format. But before writing anything, look at what you need to communicate and why.

## WHY WRITE?

Before you write anything, you must determine if there is a need to write. Ask yourself these questions:

- *Do you want a written record?*
- *Is there a need to be absolutely sure you are being complete?*
- *Do you want the reader to have a document to refer to?*
- *Has there been an established practice of writing for this purpose (invitations, etc.)?*
- *Have you been requested to reply in writing?*
- *Do you want to take time for thought or research?*

If the answer to any of these questions is *yes*, then write.

### When Not to Write

There are instances when writing a letter or memo is *not* the best way to handle communication. To determine when it is best to use the telephone or make a personal visit, ask yourself these questions.

- *Do you need an answer right away?*
- *Would you like to hear or see reactions of the recipient?*
- *Is there a likelihood of dialogue?*

If the answer to any of these questions is *yes*, then a call or visit would be more effective. In addition, if you answered *yes* to questions in both lists it may be advisable to make a call or visit and then write a letter confirming what was said.

After you answer these questions, you'll know why you're writing. But before you start, give some attention to the basics of good writing, the five C's. You'll want to keep them in mind whatever and whenever you write.

## THE FIVE C's

All good business communications have five characteristics in common. Let them be your guide in preparing letters, memos and reports, and you will find you are turning out professional work.

Effective communications are:

- *Clear*
- *Concise*

- *Complete*
- *Considerate*
- *Comprehensible*

Here's how you can achieve each of these communication goals.

## Make It *Clear*

To make sure that your writing is understandable to the reader, have a clear understanding yourself of what you want to say, organize your ideas into a logical pattern (e.g., chronological, order of importance, etc.), and use proper wording and mechanics. Here are some ideas to keep in mind.

• **Careful planning.** Have a firm grasp of what you are setting out to accomplish and a plan for how to achieve it. Focus everything on the desired result.

• **Well organized ideas.** Present your ideas in a sequence that is appropriate to your use inductive or deductive reasoning, cause and effect, pro and con, logic, chronology, or ascending or descending order of importance.

• **Proper wording.** The simpler, the better. Don't try to impress people with your stunning vocabulary. Instead, impress them with how directly you can communicate an idea. *Talk* to the reader; picture the person in front of you. Your writing will improve if you read your words out loud. If they sound artificial, try to find more natural-sounding alternatives.

• **Proper mechanics.** Double-check your writing for proper punctuation, paragraphing and other mechanical items. It's amazing what a few misplaced commas or run-on sentences can do to muddy the communication waters. (See Appendix II for a review of punctuation rules.)

A technique for checking clarity (aside from having another person read your draft) is to pretend that you are not familiar with the situation being covered in the letter. Put yourself in your reader's shoes and see if you can understand the communication. Keep revising it until you feel it simply cannot be misconstrued.

## Make It *Concise*

Whenever you begin a business letter, report, or memo, you should remember that your reader will, in all probability, be eager to get through it as quickly as possible. Long-winded writing is likely to annoy your readers, lose their interest, and even confuse them. You must be complete (see below), but you should also try to be concise. Follow these suggestions.

• **State your ideas in as few words as possible.** No one wants to read ten sentences when two will do. However, be sure you're not sacrificing clarity or completeness.

• **Use one-word expressions instead of trite phrases.** (See Appendix I for suggestions.)

- **Come right to the point.** Omit standard—but deadweight—beginnings such as "Responding to your letter of ...."
- **Keep sentences relatively short.** This aids both brevity and clarity.

## Make It *Complete*

Give the reader all the data needed to comply with your request or evaluate the situation. You can double-check yourself by:

- **Reviewing the request** or assignment you have received to make sure that you are including all the requested information.
- **Making a list of the required items** and checking them off as you include them in draft. (Check the final letter against this list, too.)
- **Getting another person to read the letter** to see if they can understand the issues, actions and information.
- **Giving sufficient background** in the letter or document. If possible, your reader should should be able to respond without having to refer elsewhere. (This will not always be feasible, especially in technical matters. In such situations, it is often a good idea to tell your readers where they can find whatever additional data they may need.) If a lot of complex data is involved, consider a one-page "Management Summary" to start off the report.

## Make It *Considerate*

In writing, as in every other form of communication, it is always important to consider the feelings of those who will be reading your words. *Consideration* for the feelings of others combined with *sincerity* will result in a document that rings true. This is seldom an easy task; don't worry if it takes a while to achieve. Just practice saying what you mean, but saying it kindly. Here are some hints to help you:

- **Picture the other person as you write.** You will be less likely to write something you wouldn't say in person.
- **Phrase your letter in a personal, rather than a corporate manner.** Say "you" "your firm"—it will add warmth.
- **When you owe the reader an apology, give one**. But don't apologize for doing something which was justified, even if it was unpleasant for the recipient.
- **Put yourself in the reader's shoes.** You will automatically add grace to your style—particularly when you must refuse something.
- **Never lecture.** Don't talk down to your reader.
- **Avoid words that have a negative ring.** Words such as *failed, demand, neglected, complaint,* etc., are likely to arouse the reader's combativeness. Less threatening expressions are more likely to encourage cooperation.

- **Explain your refusals.** Get the reader to feel, *I would have done the same thing.*

## Make It *Comprehensible*

A good newspaper or magazine tries to make its format "inviting." Good business writing should do the same thing. Following is a list of techniques used by professionals.

- **Use headings and subheadings.** Divide up your work, especially when you are dealing with lengthy or complex ideas. You can further distinguish between major and minor headings by using ALL CAPITAL letters, or indenting more than usual. (You can also use "outline" numbers and letters, such as I., A., 1., etc.)

- **Leave lots of white space** in the layout of the correspondence. An uncramped letter or report is much easier to read.

- **Use transitions** between paragraphs that draw the reader into the next idea by linking it to the previous one. Words like *however, on the other hand, conversely, similarly, moreover* or phrases expressing these ideas will pull the reader along.

- **Keep the reader in mind**, directing your writing to the reader's interests.

- **Choose your words carefully** with readability as your goal. Stick to the simple, the fresh, the direct. Add personality and persuasiveness to your letters by using fresh expressions, but guard against using words simply for effect.

- **Make sure the final letter is proofread thoroughly** for typographical, spelling, grammatical errors. These detract from the finished product's attractiveness and effectiveness.

When your writing is clear, concise, complete, considerate, and comprehensible, you will have accomplished your goal.

The five C's: Keep them in mind in all your writing; if one is missing, your message will not get through. Now let's turn to the actual writing.

Chapter 2

# How to Write—
# The Five-step System

Writing needn't be overwhelming. Use this easy to follow five-step plan to simplify all your writing tasks. This plan works with all types of writing from interoffice memos to management reports so you can use it every day. The easy steps to follow are:

**1. Plan.** Learn what information you need to have before you begin to write.

**2. Determine the format.** Discover how the way in which you present your information influences the effectiveness of your writing.

**3. Outline.** Use this quick easy way to sort out all the information you need to convey.

**4. Write.** Learn how to actually put your thoughts into writing.

**5. Edit.** Double-check to feel confident and appear professional.

When you follow these simple five steps, you get the job done in less time because you know what you need to complete the job, and you have a plan of attack. You don't have to worry that you will forget something because the steps are here in black and white, all you have to do is follow them. Let's get started right at the beginning with *planning*.

## PLAN

Planning is all important. There are few people—even professional writers—who can sit down and write without planning. Before you start writing the actual letter, memo or report, you should plan it carefully and in detail. Planning will give you better results and save you time. Moreover, it makes the actual writing task much easier. Think of it as using a road map in unfamiliar territory; it is so much faster and easier than guessing what is around the next corner.

Your plan should take two things into consideration:
1. What is my task?
2. Who is my reader?

## What Is the Task to Be Accomplished?

Carefully analyze exactly what you want to accomplish.

Are you requesting something? And if so, is it of major or minor importance to the person receiving the request? Either way, you will have to convince them that it is worth their while to grant your request. If you are merely imparting information or responding positively to a request of theirs, your task is easier—but don't miss the chance to build goodwill with your response. Are you recommending a course of action? Then you will have to structure a good argument to gain acceptance. Show your readers how adopting your plan of action will benefit them.

Must you turn down a request? If so, you should try to maintain good relations despite your inability to grant the request. Tactfully explain why you cannot cooperate, and, if possible, suggest an alternative which may be of help.

Are you writing a report? Then you must simplify data and present it in an understandable, organized manner.

### Requesting and Recommending

Here is where your powers of persuasion and positive thinking will be called into play. Some points to consider are:

- **Show what's in it for the reader.** Decide what the reader will get out of granting your request or following your recommendation. Let the reader know delicately what the benefit for the reader is. (Wouldn't you be wondering the same thing?)

- **Adopt a positive attitude**. Assume that the person will grant your request.

- **Justify your request.** Let the reader know why you want cooperation and what is at stake.

- **Reassure the reader.** If there are drawbacks to cooperating with you, state that you will do all you can to minimize any negative repercussions.

- **State what you want** from the reader. List all the things needed to grant your request.

- **Make responding convenient.** Making it easy for the reader to comply will speed up the the reply.

## Saying *Yes*

Obviously, saying yes to a request is the most pleasant writing task you will have. Plans for a good *yes* letter should include the following:

- **A list of the things you want to cover.** Be thorough but concise. Include only what is needed to answer the question or grant the request, and organize it well.

- **A sincere effort to build goodwill**, since the reader will be in a positive frame of mind when receiving a *yes* letter. Sometimes this can be as simple as mentioning how glad you are to be of help.

- **An attempt to establish the right tone**. It should be warm and helpful, not condescending.

## Saying *No*

Naturally saying *no* is not as pleasant a task as saying *yes*, but careful thought before writing will make it easier and as gracious as it can be. Your task is two-fold: to refuse a request and yet maintain goodwill. Consider the following:

- **The validity of the request**. Assume that the writer had a good reason for making the request, even if your initial reaction was negative. Adopting this frame of mind costs you nothing, but could pay off in added goodwill from the person being refused. You are going to say *no* anyway, so why not make an effort to be respectful and pleasant?

- **A good reason for not granting the request**. You want the reader to conclude that anyone in your shoes would respond the same way, so your reasoning should be sound.

- **The approach you will use.** For example, should you say *no* right off, or lead up to the refusal by laying groundwork first?

- **Any alternatives you can suggest.** How can you help the reader in light of your refusal of the request?

## Presenting Information

When there is a need to present information in the form of a report, the greatest concerns should be organizing the information into a logical format and keeping the report simple and clear. To accomplish this, just keep in mind the guidelines to good communication presented in this Section and follow the outline of a business report in Section III.

By following these guidelines, your report will express exactly what you want it to in a professional manner.

## Writing Social Letters

There are many occasions which require you to invite business associates to a social event, reply to a social invitation, or express gratitude. These are usually done in standard forms. See Section II for samples of social letters.

Now that you know exactly what task you need to accomplish, the next essential consideration is the reader. Who will be on the receiving end?

## Who Is the Reader?

This means more than just knowing the name of the recipient. You have to know two things: your reader's personality and your reader's likely reaction to what you have to say.

First, your reader's personality. Do you know what he or she will like? Is she a no-nonsense type who resists anything that doesn't look official—even scientific? Is he an informal type who would regard such an approach as stuffy? If you know for certain, then your task is that much easier. You can tailor your writing to meet your reader's expectations.

What do you do when you don't know the reader? What approach you should take? The answer to that question is easy. You are *always* better off adopting a formal, businesslike style. There is a slight risk that you will be seen as stuffy, but this is minimal compared to the damage that can be done if an informal letter or report is received by someone who regards it as unprofessional.

Second, you have to think about how your reader is going to react to what you have to say. Is the news good or bad? Are you doing a favor or asking for one? Will your reader be glad to see the answer (or proposition)? Or do you have to soften the blow? What is the best way to convince the reader to accept your idea? Think about personality—tailor your message to appeal to the reader's outlook, and it will be accepted more readily. Think about the position and level of understanding of the recipient—how basic (or technical) must you be to make sure that your message is understood? Determine at what level you should gear your presentation as not to insult or appear condescending to your reader. Also consider the reader's perspective and goals—and how does your idea impact those goals? In sum, look at the total picture surrounding your reader. Target your message to the interests, goals and disposition of the reader.

# DETERMINE THE FORMAT

Once you've planned your project, you know what you want to say. The next step is to decide how you want to present it. Using the proper style and form for your correspondence will add to its impact. Think of the image you want to project and select a style that reflects that image best. (Note that styles of reports are covered in Section III. Here we will concentrate on letters and memos.)

## Things to Consider

Here are three things to consider as you select the format and style that you will use:

- **Formality.** Do you know the recipient? well? casually? at all? Are you writing to a co-worker? a familiar client? a prospective client?
- **Company standards.** Is there a standard procedure for in-house correspondence? outside correspondence? Are you representing your company to an outsider?
- **Purpose.** What is the purpose of the correspondence? Is it just to impart information from department to department or is it a document that will be kept and referred to?

The answers to the above questions should give you an idea of the proper style to use when writing. Common sense will help, too. Naturally, writing a letter proposing a three-year deal with a new customer requires more formality than a note to a co-worker that the monthly production meeting has been postponed.

## Styles of Writing

There are three basic styles of writing: formal, semiformal, and familiar. No matter what your project is, there are at least three ways to present your information. Formal, semiformal, and familiar styles can be used for letters, memos and reports. Basically you determine which to use by asking the questions above and by considering what the purpose of the document is.

### Formal

Use the formal style when writing to someone you don't know outside your organization, a superior, or unfamiliar vendor, a client, etc.; or when the purpose of the document demands it, (e.g., proposal, contract). The formal style should also be used when the document will be used as a record (e.g., company policy, discipline, commendation).

Physical presentation is also important when you are trying to project a certain image. When writing a formal letter, it should be done in a full block or semiblock style. Generally, the block style is characterized by "open" punctuation. That means no punctuation after the date line, address, and signature.

All formal letters are typewritten (or produced on a word processor and printed on a letter-quality printer). A sample of a formal letter of recommendation follows. Notice that it is reserved and distant in tone.

# Formal

June 1, 1986

John Marsh, Personnel Manager
Union Manufacturing Company
1 Main Street
Fairport, New York

Dear Mr. Marsh:

I am pleased to recommend Rose Stephens for promotion to Assistant Production Director. Ms. Stephens was my administrative assistant from 1981 through 1985. She has been a conscientious, knowledgeable and pleasant-natured employee. Her sharp eye for detail was balanced by an ability to grasp the overall concept of a project. She consistently performed her duties in a timely, thorough fashion, and frequently took the initiative to do more than was required.

She is clearly ready for promotion to Assistant Product Director, and we regret that we do not have such a promotion for her at this time. We understand her desire to advance as quickly as possible, and, therefore, wish her success in her search for a challenging position outside this organization.

Sincerely yours,

### Semiformal

Use a semiformal style when writing to co-workers and persons outside the organization when the correspondence requires professional treatment of the subject matter without the distance of a strictly formal letter. A full block, block, or semiblock style is used, but a more familiar tone distinguishes it from a formal letter. A sample of a semiformal letter follows. Note that the language of the letter is now more relaxed, though not as friendly as the familiar style.

## Semiformal

June 1, 1986

John Marsh
Personnel Manager
Union Manufacturing Company
1 Main Street
Fairport, New York

Dear Mr. Marsh,

I am pleased to recommend Rose Stephens to you for the position of Assistant Production Director. She has been a conscientious worker in my department for the past four years, taking care of the details of our projects as well as keeping the projects focused and on target. She is a hard worker, frequently taking the initiative and doing more than was expected of her.

She is clearly ready for promotion to Assistant Production Director. If we had an opening to offer her, we would. Please call me if you want to discuss this further.

Sincerely,

**Familiar**

Use a familiar style when writing a note or letter to someone you know. A sample of a familiar letter follows. Obviously the tone and style are much more relaxed and convivial than the other two styles. It will be helpful to think how the recipient will use the correspondence. Will it be shown to others? Will it be a permanent record?

## Familiar

June 1, 1986

Dear John,

    I hear that you are looking for someone to fill Jim's place. My administrative assistant, Rose Stephens, would be great for that job. As you know, she has been with me for four years, and I feel she's ready for a promotion. She's a hard worker and keeps our office running smoothly even when I'm out. I would hate to see her go but she really has potential for that assistant product director position.

    Call me if you're interested, and I'll give you more information.

    Yours,

**Memos**

Interoffice memos are used for intracompany communications. While memo forms vary slightly from company to company, most follow the format illustrated below. With the exception of salutations and complimentary closes, memos should be planned and written like business letters.

In addressing memos, most companies alphabetize multiple recipients to avoid the sensitive issue of rank. If you wish one copy of the memo to circulate among several people, place a "please route" notation after the "To." Employees will read, initial or cross off their names, and pass the memo on to the next person on the list. If you want someone to get a copy simply for information purposes—not action—place "FYI" (For Your Information) next to the name. Memos are generally signed at the bottom or initialed next to the "From" name. A sample memo appears below.

## Memo

```
Date:   November 1, 1985

To:   Ms. Doe

From:   Ralph Smith

Re:   Budget for First Quarter, 1986

Please prepare a budget summary on your account, X-O Soap,
for the First Quarter of 1986.  Include production, media
and research costs, broken down by month.  I would like the
budget by November 15.  Call if you have any questions.
                                             (Signed)
```

Now that we have gone through Step One—Planning and Step Two—Determining the Format, let's move on to Step Three—Outlining.

# OUTLINE

Most people shy away from writing an outline unless they are writing a detailed report. They think that an outline is a lot of work. They do not realize that an outline could *save* them a great deal of work *and* help produce a clear, concise document.

An outline does not have to be a formal document. Simply write down the most important thing you have to tell your reader; reduce everything you need to convey into one sentence. Then decide the most appropriate order to present your information to get the desired result. Underneath the main statement, write all the important supporting facts leaving room between each one to put supporting information, keeping in mind the order (e.g., order of importance, chronological order). At the end put a sentence stating what you would like the reader to remember after reading your document. Formal conclusions are not always necessary. If your document is a memo or short letter, omit the conclusion. On the other hand, reports and long letters require that you restate your message at the end so that there is no confusion as to your exact intentions.

Read over your outline filling in any gaps and checking the order. *That's all there is to it.*

This step organizes your information into manageable sections and makes sure you will get your main point across first, followed by your supporting details in a logical order. This procedure will force you to think about how you are going to justify your request or support your findings. You cannot forget important details in writing your document if you complete an outline. Another advantage of doing an outline is identifying areas in which you need to compile more information or use persuasive language.

Following is the outline that was written to compose the sample formal letter presented in the previous section. You can see that it organizes the information so that the writer has an easier time writing the actual letter.

## Outline

Main Statement: I am pleased to recommend Rose Stephens for promotion to assistant product director.

1. Reasons I think she would be qualified.
   (Ascending order of importance)
   - She has been a good worker for four years.
   - She is conscientious, knowledgeable and pleasant-natured.
   - She has a sharp eye for detail.
   - She can grasp the overall concept of a project.
   - She is on time.
   - She is thorough.
   - She frequently takes the initiative to do more than required.

2. How we feel about promoting her
   - We regret that we do not have a promotion to offer her.

- We understand her desire to advance as quickly as possible.
- We wish her success.

You probably would not take valuable time to type out such a neat formal outline, because many letters and memos do not require it. It is presented as a format for longer more complex letters and reports and to show you the organization of thoughts in preparing the letter. The following represents what you might have actually had on your notepad before writing this letter.

## Notes

*Recommendation - Rose*
- *Good worker*
- *4 years experience*
- *eye for detail*
- *punctual*
- *thorough*
- *has initiative*
- *we don't have a promotion to offer*

# WRITE

Now that you've considered the five C's, evaluated the task and the reader, selected the approach and written an outline, you're ready to *write*. This stage will go quickly if you have planned your correspondence and use the guidelines that follow.

## Guidelines

Following the guidelines presented below will simplify your task. Each time you have an occasion to write, quickly go through the list and determine if you have addressed every issue.

- **Get to the point right away.** A subject line accomplishes this immediately.

```
John Doe
1 Main Street
Fairport, New York

Dear Mr. Doe:

     I am happy to report the findings of our latest survey
of customer preferences.
```

- **Gain the reader's interest.** Think of the first part of a letter or report as an advertising headline. A headline tries to get the reader's attention, either by promising a benefit or arousing curiosity. For example, if you are writing a report on affirmative action and the news is good, don't hesitate to trumpet the fact in your first sentence. You might be tempted to begin the report with a long, involved history of the AA program, but if you do, your readers are likely to be asleep by the time you tell them that you have more than exceeded your goals during the last period.
- **When possible, begin with a compliment or favorable comment about the reader.** Caution: Make sure that it is natural and sincere; if not, omit it.

```
John Doe
1 Main Street
Fairport, New York

Dear Mr. Doe:

     I enjoyed meeting with you last week.
```

- **Be positive.** Start with the good news and point out positive aspects of unfavorable news.
- **Use *you*, not *we* or *I*.** You gain attention by addressing the reader right away, not by talking about yourself or your company. Focus on the reader.
- **Show that you are aware of the problem or situation.** Identify and describe it immediately; don't leave your reader hanging. Make it clear you understand. You will gain respect and be in a position to demand action if you are seen as fully informed.
- **Explain in detail your purpose in writing.** Don't let the reader guess. Spell out the reason you are writing.

- **Be complete.** Make sure you cover everything. When you leave out vital information, you may lose respect in the reader's eyes. In addition, precious time will be lost while the reader tries to fill in the gaps. In some cases no action on the issue can take place without all the facts.

- **Explain what you want.** Be sure it's clear what you want the reader to do.

- **Follow the Five C's** of good writing to ensure that the point you intend to make gets across. Check yourself to see that what you're writing is clear, concise, complete, considerate and comprehensible. Don't stray from the subject or go into unnecessary detail.

- **Finish as soon as possible.** Do not ramble on.

- **Leave the reader with a favorable impression.** It will promote goodwill.

- **Offer help** or further information if you are serious about providing it. Don't sign off with "If I can be of further assistance . . ." unless you really mean it.

- **Recap** what you want done, when you want it, and how the reader can go about it—in other words, end with a "call to action."

- **End on a personal note, if appropriate.** You may need to reassure, compliment, express express appreciation, or make a friendly personal comment.

## Writing

Now you're ready to start actually writing your document! Since you've prepared fully for this, the blank piece of paper is not so frightening. You know what your objective is. You know what you need to say and how you need to say it to accomplish your objective.

All you need to do is take the outline you have prepared and expand it into coherent paragraphs. In your first paragraph let the reader know what the purpose of the document is. If you are reporting your findings of an investigation, say so. If you are recommending a former employee to a prospective employer, state this first. Use the first statement that you wrote on your outline. Then state in general terms what you are going to present in the rest of the document. Then write each supporting fact, in the order you have decided upon when writing your outline. Expand each section of your outline so that you have complete thoughts that follow logically from one to another. After you have written down all the supporting data, again follow your outline and recap and state what you want the reader to remember. You have just written your first draft!

After writing your first draft, leave it alone for a while if time allows. When you come back to it, you will have a fresh approach. Read over your document in its entirety without interruption. Look for abrupt breaks in continuity, completeness, a logical flow of information, and a consistent tone. Do not at this point look for misspellings or correct margins, etc. Fix any major problems right away (if you are interrupted, jot down what the problems are so you won't be repeating your efforts). Then reprint or retype your document with the changes and read it over again. This time, in addition to checking the new changes to see if they are consistent in flow and tone with the rest of the document, use the writing guideline checklist below to check over your document. Also look for correct punctuation, spelling, and grammar. Check the layout to see if it is appropriate and done correctly. Incorporate all these changes into the document and reprint or retype it again.

**Note for Writers Who Dictate**

This step-by-step preparation is especially valuable to those who dictate their correspondence. When dictating, use your outline the same way you would if you were writing. Expand each point indicated on your outline in the sequence you've decided on, and you will be assured that the result will be a coherent, organized document.

**Note for Writers with Word Processors**

If you are using a word processor, your job will be considerably shorter since you need only type the document once. Making changes and corrections on the computer eliminates the retyping step. Some writers like editing "on screen" while others prefer to have "hard copy" printed out for editing. The important point is, make your technology work *for* you.

**Note for Writers with Secretaries**

Your secretary can be a great asset—the best of them are great proofreaders. Your secretary will have an easier time if you follow the procedures here carefully. That way you may avoid having documents typed over and over because they weren't carefully organized and outlined.

Now you are ready for the last step!

# EDIT

Good editing can make the difference between writing that embarrasses and that which enhances a career. Read your final draft and double-check for factual, grammatical, and stylistic errors. Editing is a necessary part of writing; *don't skip it!* One error could mean loss of support or even complete failure of a project.

## Looking It Over

How do you go about editing your writing? Simply:

• **Make sure you have included everything.** Check your outline, old drafts, notes, or the letter to which you are responding.

• **Check for a logical flow throughout.** Is it easy to follow or do you jump from another?

- **Double-check any facts and figures.** Erroneous data is probably the worst thing that your reader can discover.
- **See if the tone is consistent.** This helps you get results from this correspondence as well as generate goodwill for future dealings.
- **Check construction and grammar.** Ask a co-worker you trust if you aren't sure.

## Appearance Is Important

The look of your correspondence and reports—as well as the content—is a reflection on you. People can't help but form opinions of you and your company from your correspondence. It's a simple matter to ensure that their impressions are favorable by making your correspondence neat-looking and letter-perfect. It tells them that you care about your work and care about them, too.

When reviewing final copy, ask yourself:
- Is there good use of white space?
- Does the letter look inviting?
- Are there any typographical errors?
- Is the layout appropriate and pleasing?

For more information on editing, see Chapter 8.

When you have finished, use the accompanying checklist to check over your writing project.

## Conclusion

Now you know how easy it is to produce an effective document. You know the five C's of effective writing and you've used the BLR Five-step System to complete your writing task. You can use these basics on *any writing task*. The next section presents samples of the most common writing tasks you face. These samples in combination with the basic writing guidelines presented in this chapter ensure that you will produce an effective professional document.

# WRITING CHECKLIST

|  | Yes | No |
|---|---|---|
| Did you get to the point? | ☐ | ☐ |
| Did you gain the reader's interest? | ☐ | ☐ |
| Did you begin with a compliment or favorable comment? | ☐ | ☐ |
| Is your writing phrased in a positive way? | ☐ | ☐ |
| Did you use *you*? | ☐ | ☐ |
| Did you show that you are aware of the problem or situation? | ☐ | ☐ |
| Did you explain your purpose in writing? | ☐ | ☐ |
| Are you sure you're being complete? | ☐ | ☐ |
| Did you explain what you want? | ☐ | ☐ |
| Did you follow the Five C's? | ☐ | ☐ |
| Did you finish it as soon as possible? | ☐ | ☐ |
| Did you leave a favorable impression? | ☐ | ☐ |
| Did you offer help? | ☐ | ☐ |
| Did you recap? | ☐ | ☐ |
| Did you end on a personal note? | ☐ | ☐ |
| Did you include everything necessary? | ☐ | ☐ |
| Did you check for a logical flow throughout? | ☐ | ☐ |
| Did you double-check any facts and figures? | ☐ | ☐ |
| Did you see if the tone is consistent? | ☐ | ☐ |
| Did you check construction and grammar? | ☐ | ☐ |
| Is there good use of white space? | ☐ | ☐ |
| Does the letter look inviting? | ☐ | ☐ |
| Are there any typographical errors? | ☐ | ☐ |
| Is the layout appropriate and pleasing? | ☐ | ☐ |

# Section II
# Sample Letters and Memos

# HOW TO USE THIS SECTION

This section contains sample letters and memos ready for your immediate use. All you have to do is fill in the underscored parts with your own information, and you will have a professional letter ready to go. Please note that most letters are preceded by a list of items which should be included in the letter. These lists should be particularly useful as you become more skilled at writing. Eventually you will begin to construct your own letters, reflecting more of your personality. Even then, lists and sample letters presented here will ensure that your correspondence maintains that all-important element: professionalism.

The topics that follow are arranged in a chronological sequence, starting with recruiting, and moving on to employing, motivating an employee, and garnering goodwill for the firm. Finally, an administrative section is included, covering daily letter writing tasks. The sections include:

- Recruitment
- Employment issues
- Motivation
- Personal touches
- Administration

Here is a list of the samples contained in Section II.

## Recruitment

Advertising for Job Openings
- Display ads.................................................................... 27
- Classified Ads................................................................ 29

Setting up Applicant Interviews ........................................... 30
Declining an Interview ........................................................ 31
Accepting an Applicant ....................................................... 32
Turning Down an Applicant ................................................. 33
Welcome to New Employee ................................................ 34
Orientation .......................................................................... 35

## Employment Issues

Recommendations/References ........................................... 37
Verification of Employment ................................................. 40
Credit References ............................................................... 41
Personnel Evaluations
- Evaluation Checklist for Clerical Positions............................ 43
- Evaluation Checklist for Managerial Positions...................... 44
- Writing Skills Guidelines...................................................... 46

*Business Writing Made Simple*

## Motivation

Special Recognition
    For Civic Service.................................................................................................. 47
    For Professional Honor....................................................................................... 48
    To an employee for a Job Well Done................................................................. 48
Goodwill
    To Employees at Year End................................................................................. 49
    To Customer, Newly Promoted........................................................................... 49

## Personal Touches

Announcements
    Birth of First Child............................................................................................... 51
    Birth of Subsequent Children............................................................................. 51
    For Adoption........................................................................................................ 52
Announcement of Retirement
    To Employee....................................................................................................... 52
    To Company........................................................................................................ 53
    Letter to Customers............................................................................................ 53
Invitation, Formal
    Issuing.................................................................................................................. 55
    Accepting............................................................................................................. 56
    Declining.............................................................................................................. 56
Invitations, Informal
    Issuing.................................................................................................................. 57
    Accepting............................................................................................................. 57
    Declining.............................................................................................................. 57
Invitations, Letterhead ............................................................................................. 58
Condolences
    To Business Associate of trhe Deceased........................................................ 59
    To a Widow(er) of an Employee........................................................................ 59
    Upon Personal Injury or Illness.......................................................................... 59
Fund Raising ............................................................................................................. 60

## Administration

Acknowledging Letters Received in Co-Workers Absence .................................. 61
Confirmations ............................................................................................................ 63
Authorizations ........................................................................................................... 64
Initiating Work ........................................................................................................... 65
Letters of Transmittal ............................................................................................... 66
Requesting Information ............................................................................................ 67
Requesting Reservations ......................................................................................... 68
Requesting a Speaker .............................................................................................. 69
Minutes ...................................................................................................................... 70

# Chapter 3

# Recruitment

## ADVERTISING FOR JOB OPENINGS

Newspaper advertising for job openings takes one of two forms: display or classified. The former is usually about four inches square, and requires artwork and/or a "mechanical," meaning that artwork and typesetting, ready for production, must be prepared and delivered to the paper. Given the time and expense involved, these advertisements are generally reserved for managerial, technical, or other more experienced personnel. Classified ads, frequently called "want ads," are the more commonly used format for recruiting clerical, secretarial and accounting personnel.

### Display Ads

In planning a display ad, keep the following factors in mind:

- The ad must be eye-catching. It must appeal to the particular audience of job seekers that you are trying to reach. The best advice we can give is this:
  - Keep the graphics simple. Don't try to be too clever, unless you have proven your graphic skills before.
  - Make it clear what you're looking for. Job seekers scan the ads, looking for "their" job. If your headline clearly defines the position you are seeking to fill, you'll be certain to attract the greatest possible number of qualified applicants.
- List the qualifications for the position, along with any restrictions/requirements (such as "must relocate" or "50% travel overseas"). Be sure not to include any discriminatory restrictions such as sex, race or age. If in doubt, check your language with your firm's legal department before submitting it to the paper.
- List any benefits which would motivate well-qualified individuals to apply.

- When a salary is mentioned, you can either give a figure or a range. When none is given, a phrase such as "salary commensurate with qualifications" can be used.
- Give the reader instructions on how to apply. Depending on your company policy, you may have applicants contact your personnel department directly by phone or letter and submit a resume, or have them respond to a box number at the paper. The latter method allows you to prescreen applicants anonymously and avoids an onslaught of calls. When the company is not identified, you should include a few words describing the firm (manufacturing or service, consumer goods or industrial, domestic or international) and its location.

Use the following display ad copy as a guideline. If services are available or you can afford to go "outside," the newspaper or an advertising agency can help with layout, type style, etc. Your copy should be submitted typed as shown, with the headline and body copy designated.

```
HEADLINE:              SALES REPRESENTATIVE
                   NEW TERRITORY—HIGH VISIBILITY


BODY COPY: Acme Products, Inc., one of the nation's fastest
           growing consumer product manufacturers, has an
           excellent opportunity for a Sales Representative
           in the NW District.  You would be based in
           Portland, Oregon and responsible for a five-
           state area.  This is Acme's newest market, and
           it offers a chance for high visibility.

           The successful candidate must be aggressive,
           with three to five years' experience in consumer
           sales and a bachelor's degree.  Salary is
           commensurate with experience.  Liberal
           commission and bonus plan, plus profit sharing.
           Other benefits include: car, expense account,
           and 100% company-paid life, medical and dental
           insurance.

           If you are a self-starter and want to join a
           winning team, send resume and salary history to:

                    Ms. A. G. Doe
                 Personnel Department
                 Acme Products, Inc.
                   112 Main Street
                  Appleton, WI 55445
              *An Equal Opportunity Employer*
```

## Classified Ads

Classified ads should be short, to the point and businesslike.

Include:

- Job title/description and type of firm. Location is optional.
- Experience—skills required (educational or on-the-job).
- Anything of special appeal or critical importance (glamorous industry, meeting the public, etc.).
- How to apply (phone for appointment, send resume, etc.).
- Name and address or phone number to contact; box number at paper if blind ad.
- Salary may or may not be mentioned.

Examples of commonly advertised positions follow.

### For Secretary

```
          SECRETARY
Prestigious nonprofit agency.
Excellent opportunity for
experienced secretary with good
typing and steno to work for
executive in congenial front office.
556-7709, Ms. Doe.
```

### For Accounting

```
        JUNIOR ACCOUNTANT
Entry level position for ambitious
accounting graduate with rapidly
expanding consumer products
manufacturer, Acme Products.
Call:    Ms. Doe, 465-7958.
```

## SETTING UP APPLICANT INTERVIEWS

When inviting job applicants to come in for an interview, be sure to include the following information in the letter:

- The position for which the firm is interviewing.
- The name, title and location (if necessary) of the person who will be conducting the interview.
- The date and time of the interview, plus a mention of whom to contact if the applicant must change the appointment.
- A request that the applicant call beforehand to confirm the appointment.
- A mention of any materials which the applicant should bring to the interview.
- A pleasant closing—a nice touch which may help to put the applicant at ease.

Dear Ms. Doe:

Mr. Fix of the Acme Personnel Agency has recommended you for the position of clerk/typist in our Personnel Department. Would it be convenient for you to come in for an interview with Ms. Black, Head of Office Services, on Thursday, January 5, at 10 a.m.? Her office is located on the fifth floor, number 21.

Please confirm this appointment with me by calling 222-2222. We are looking forward to meeting you, as Mr. Fix had nice things to say about you.

Sincerely,

## DECLINING AN INTERVIEW

When you receive unsolicited applications for employment and must decline a requested interview, try to make your response tactful. After all, when a position does become available, you may want to interview the very person you are currently turning away. Think of this letter as an opportunity to create goodwill for your company. This should make the task of having to turn down an applicant's interview request easier. The worst thing to do is not to respond at all. It is rude to the applicant and potentially damaging to the firm's reputation.

Points to include in such a letter are:

- Thank the applicant for showing interest in the firm.
- Explain that there are no openings at this time.
- If appropriate, state that the application will be kept on file in case an opening does develop.

Dear Ms. Doe:

We were pleased to learn of your interest in joining Acme Products as a cost accountant. Your letter indicates that you have had some solid experience in the field and are probably a well-qualified candidate. However, I regret to tell you that we have no openings for cost accountants at this time. Therefore, we will be unable to interview you now, but will be sure to keep you in mind should an opening develop.

Thank you for again for thinking of us, Ms. Doe.

Sincerely,

*Business Writing Made Simple*

## ACCEPTING AN APPLICANT

This is one of the more enjoyable letters you will have occasion to write. It contains good news for the recipient and the company. Fresh beginnings deserve a bright tone. Items in this letter should include:

- Title or description of the position being offered.
- Date and time the employment is to commence. Note the location and person to whom to report on the first day.
- Anything the new employee should bring with him.
- Statement of the salary which was agreed upon. (A complete listing of benefits may be included in this or it can wait for orientation.)
- A note of welcome to the new employee.


Dear Ms. Doe:

I am delighted to offer you the position of <u>Administrative Assistant</u> <u>to the Personnel Manager</u>. <u>Ms. Black</u> was very impressed with your qualifications, as was I. We hope you decide to join <u>Acme Products</u>.

Call us by <u>August 5th</u> to let us know your decision. We will hope to see you on <u>August 10</u> at <u>8:30 a.m.</u> in <u>Ms. Black's office</u>. Please bring a small recent photograph for your identification card.

As we agreed, the annual salary will be <u>$15,000</u>, <u>with a six-month review</u>. You will be eligible for <u>two weeks'</u> paid vacation after one year of service.

All of us in the personnel department are looking forward to working with you, Ms. Doe. We think you will like it here!

Sincerely,

## TURNING DOWN AN APPLICANT

Tact is of prime concern in drafting a letter to inform an applicant who has been unsuccessful in getting the position for which they interviewed. To soften the blow, a kind comment about the applicant should be included, along with thanks for considering the company as a potential employer.

The letter should include:
- Phrasing which is as supportive as possible.
- Positive statements about the good points of the person's qualifications.
- A brief statement explaining why the applicant was rejected.
- Thanks for considering the company.
- A wish for future success in finding a good job.

Dear Ms. Doe:

Thank you for interviewing with us last Thursday. We were all very impressed with your academic background, and are convinced that you will do very well when you enter the world of business.

While you show a great deal of potential, we have decided to offer the position to a candidate whose qualifications more closely match our particular needs.

Thank you for considering Acme Products, Ms. Doe. We enjoyed meeting you, and we wish you much luck in your career.

Sincerely,

*Business Writing Made Simple*

# WELCOME TO NEW EMPLOYEE

This letter offers you a chance to get the relationship between your firm and the new employee off to a good start. Optimism is the key word. You may compliment both the employee and the firm and assure the newcomer that you will both benefit from the new association. Include:

- A hearty welcome to the employee.
- A compliment on the wisdom of choosing your company.
- A confirmation of the employee's job title.
- A statement that you know the association will be successful and mutually beneficial.
- The name of a person or department to whom the new employee can turn for help/information during orientation or the first few months on the job.

The object here is to let the new employees know that you are prepared to make every effort to help them succeed.


Welcome to Acme Products, Ms. Doe!

We are delighted that you have decided to join us as <u>Plant Personnel</u> <u>Manager</u>. We know that our association will be a long and successful one.

<u>Acme</u> has been experiencing <u>unprecedented growth</u> during the past year, making your new job <u>an expanding and increasingly</u> important one. We know that you will grow with us.

You will be glad to know that <u>Mr. Smith</u>, <u>Director of Personnel</u>, will always be available to answer your questions and discuss things with you. Feel free to drop in on him any time.

If there is anything that any of us at <u>Acme Products</u> can do to help you, let us know. We are delighted to have you and want you to feel at home!

Sincerely,

# ORIENTATION

This letter deals with the "nuts and bolts" of the employment agreement. Just how much data should go into the letter will be determined by whether or not you have standardized forms or booklets dealing with employee benefits. If so, a simple letter outlining salary, vacation and insurance arrangements will suffice. Be sure to cover:

- Starting date and job title/description.
- Starting salary, plus any commission or salary review agreements.
- Insurance and health benefits. (Include policies.)
- A note of welcome to the firm.

Dear Ms. Doe:

Welcome to <u>Acme Products</u>. We are pleased that you will be joining us as <u>Plant Personnel Manager</u> as of <u>June 1, 1986</u>.

This letter will outline the benefits available to you as a new employee of <u>Acme Products</u>. (List here the type and amounts of insurance -- health and life -- available to the employee, either at the firm's expense or as a contribution by the employee.)

As we agreed in your final interview, your annual salary will be <u>$25,000</u>, payable <u>monthly</u>. Your performance will be reviewed <u>annually</u>, in accordance with the personnel policy we discussed. In addition, you can count on <u>a Christmas bonus</u>, <u>the amount to be determined on the basis of corporate performance</u>. <u>Acme</u> takes pride in sharing its profits with its valued employees!

After <u>six months</u> with <u>Acme</u>, you will be entitled to <u>one week</u> of vacation with pay. After the <u>one-year</u> anniversary, you may have <u>two weeks' paid vacation</u>, and after <u>five</u> years, you will enjoy <u>three weeks</u> of vacation.

<u>Acme</u> allows <u>two personal days per year</u>, to be taken at your discretion, plus all the major national holidays. <u>Paid sick leave</u> can amount to <u>10 days per year</u>, with longer absences subject to review.

You will find the enclosed pamphlets on <u>insurance and health benefits</u> very informative, and we request that you read them carefully. We will be glad to answer any questions on them.

Again, welcome, <u>Ms. Doe</u>.  We look forward to having your talent on the <u>Acme</u> team;  we know it will be a winning combination!

Sincerely,

# Chapter 4

# Employment Issues

## RECOMMENDATIONS/REFERENCES

This letter can present a considerable challange. It calls for a combination of honesty and tact—honesty because the letter of recommendation reflects on your ability to evaluate the performance and character of the person being recommended and tact because someone's job hangs in the balance.

Your letter carries a lot of weight, and you owe it to yourself, the addressee and the person being recommended to be truthful but diplomatic. Try to keep any personal bias out of the evaluation and to judge the person on merit—not your feelings. If there was strife between you and the employee, remember that other personality types may blend better.

There are two types of personnel recommendations—those specifically addressed to a potential employer and those going to unidentified people, referred to as "open" letters of recommendation. The former can be far more helpful to potential employers because you can respond to questions directly. You can also be a bit more candid because the employee will not see the letter. "Open" letters require a much more general approach, as they should be appropriate for different types of businesses or positions for which the employee is likely to apply.

While challenging to write, a well-written letter of recommendation can give you a great deal of satisfaction. It not only represents a very sophisticated form of business writing, but it also performs the dual role of helping your former employee find a more suitable job and cementing a feeling of goodwill among your firm, yourself and the former employee.

Following are guidelines for writing letters of recommendation:

- Wed tact with truth.
- Don't let your personal feelings color your evaluation of a person's ability or performance.
- Highlight the good points but don't ignore the bad.
- Mention the length of time the person was in your employ and the position held.
- Respond truthfully to any specific questions which a potential employer asks—unless they are inappropriate, potentially discriminatory, violate the employee's privacy, or present other legal problems.
- Be wary of making any negative comments which you cannot clearly substantiate.

Since these are difficult letters to write, three examples follow. The first is written for a former employee deserving of high praise, the second for a more problematic case, and the third is a sample "open" letter.

Dear Ms. Doe:

Responding to your letter of enquiry about the job qualifications of Sam Jackson, I am pleased to tell you that you would be hard pressed to find a better candidate for Comptroller than Sam. He was the Comptroller for Acme from 1978 through 1986, and consistently performed his job with a high degree of professionalism. He was also very well-liked by his co-workers.

Sam left us in order to seek a position which would give him broader business exposure, and I think that a firm like yours would provide him with this growth potential. While we hated to lose him, we wish him every success and think he would be a superb addition to your firm.

Sincerely,

Dear Ms. Doe,

In response to your request for a recommendation for Mr. Dee, I must honestly say that he was not with us long enough for us to get to know him or his work habits very well. However, during his brief stay (one month) he seemed to be conscientious and courteous to the customers as a Salesperson.

His higher-than-normal absenteeism was our only complaint. If Mr. Dee is able to overcome the problem, I think he would be a fine salesperson. We wish him success in his sales career.

Sincerely,

To Whom It May Concern:

Ms. Stephens was my administrative assistant from 1980 through 1986. I am pleased to recommend her as a conscientious, knowledgeable and pleasant-natured employee. Her sharp eye for detail was balanced by an ability to grasp the overall concept of a project. She consistently performed her duties in a timely, thorough fashion, and frequently took the initiative to do more than was required. She is clearly ready for promotion to an assistant product director slot, and we regret that we do not have one for her to fill just now.

We understand her desire to advance as quickly as possible, and therefore wish her success in her search for a more challenging position.

Sincerely,

## VERIFICATION OF EMPLOYMENT

This letter differs from a recommendation in scope and tone. While recommendations pass judgment on the employee's performance, verifications are merely statements about the length of the employee's service and position. Do not offer more than that, or you may be encroaching on the employee's rights.

Although verifications are usually given on the phone, when a letter is requested it should contain:

- Full name of the employee.
- Dates for start and end of employment.
- Position held.

```
Dear Ms. Doe:
This confirms that Sam Allen Doy was employed as Head of
Production and Development for Acme Products, Inc., from
April 1, 1960 to January 2, 1980.
Sincerely,
```

## CREDIT REFERENCES

From time to time you will be called upon by creditors to provide information on employees' employment records and salaries. The best policy to follow is to provide only the data requested, nothing more. When asked to supply information beyond employment dates and salary level, it is best to either decline or check with local and state laws before cooperating. Be sensitive to your workers' feelings and legal creditworthiness, or behavior. Simply provide:

- Name of employee.
- Length of time employed.
- Only when requested: salary level. (Many firms refuse to reveal this information and are within their rights in doing so.)

Dear Ms. Smith:

In response to your inquiry about John French, this confirms that he has been employed with us since March 10, 1975.

Sincerely,

## PERSONNEL EVALUATIONS

Before you can write an evaluation of an employee's performance, you must first set up the criteria for the evaluation. To do this, you must decide what constitutes "ideal" performance, then measure the employee's performance against it.

As with the recommendation letter, you must guard against letting your personal feelings toward employees color your evaluation of their job performance. Put feelings aside and deal with the concrete factors of achievement and ability. Honesty is all-important, since you will do no one a favor in the long run if you give either an unfairly positive or negative evaluation. Either way, it will catch up with them, and you. So be fair, honest and objective.

The following evaluation checklists will help you to assess an employee's performance, skills, knowledge and personal characteristics. Select the checklists which relate to the type of job you are evaluating. You may use the checklist forms either for the actual evaluation or as guidelines for developing a written evaluation.

*Employment Issues*

# EVALUATION CHECKLIST FOR CLERICAL POSITIONS

## SKILLS:

|  | Excellent | Good | Average | Needs Improvement | Unsatisfactory |
|---|---|---|---|---|---|
| Phone manner | ☐ | ☐ | ☐ | ☐ | ☐ |
| Typing |  |  |  |  |  |
|   Speed | ☐ | ☐ | ☐ | ☐ | ☐ |
|   Accuracy | ☐ | ☐ | ☐ | ☐ | ☐ |
| Stenography |  |  |  |  |  |
|   Speed | ☐ | ☐ | ☐ | ☐ | ☐ |
|   Accuracy | ☐ | ☐ | ☐ | ☐ | ☐ |
| Filing | ☐ | ☐ | ☐ | ☐ | ☐ |
| Spelling/Grammar | ☐ | ☐ | ☐ | ☐ | ☐ |
| OVERALL | ☐ | ☐ | ☐ | ☐ | ☐ |

## PERSONAL CHARACTERISTICS:

|  | Excellent | Good | Average | Needs Improvement | Unsatisfactory |
|---|---|---|---|---|---|
| Helpfulness | ☐ | ☐ | ☐ | ☐ | ☐ |
| Initiative | ☐ | ☐ | ☐ | ☐ | ☐ |
| Promptness | ☐ | ☐ | ☐ | ☐ | ☐ |
| Reliability | ☐ | ☐ | ☐ | ☐ | ☐ |
| Works well with others | ☐ | ☐ | ☐ | ☐ | ☐ |
| OVERALL | ☐ | ☐ | ☐ | ☐ | ☐ |

## POTENTIAL:                                                              Yes     No

Should be considered for promotion to office manager, administrative assistant, executive secretary, (other). (Specify position.)   ☐   ☐

____mos. Estimated number of months before candidate will be ready for the suggested promotion.

List additional training necessary for promotion.

_____

_____

_____

GENERAL COMMENTS

_____

_____

_____

*Business Writing Made Simple*

# EVALUATION CHECKLIST FOR MANAGERIAL POSITIONS

## SKILLS:

|  | Excellent | Good | Average | Needs Improvement | Unsatisfactory |
|---|---|---|---|---|---|
| Knowledge | ☐ | ☐ | ☐ | ☐ | ☐ |
| Judgment | ☐ | ☐ | ☐ | ☐ | ☐ |
| Problem Solving | ☐ | ☐ | ☐ | ☐ | ☐ |
| Planning | ☐ | ☐ | ☐ | ☐ | ☐ |
| Organization | ☐ | ☐ | ☐ | ☐ | ☐ |
| Training Subordinates | ☐ | ☐ | ☐ | ☐ | ☐ |
| Communication:* |  |  |  |  |  |
|   Written | ☐ | ☐ | ☐ | ☐ | ☐ |
|   Oral | ☐ | ☐ | ☐ | ☐ | ☐ |
| Work Habits | ☐ | ☐ | ☐ | ☐ | ☐ |
| Ability to Motivate Employees | ☐ | ☐ | ☐ | ☐ | ☐ |
| Ability to Delegate | ☐ | ☐ | ☐ | ☐ | ☐ |
| Creativity |  |  |  |  |  |
| OVERALL: | ☐ | ☐ | ☐ | ☐ | ☐ |

## PERSONAL CHARACTERISTICS:

|  | Excellent | Good | Average | Needs Improvement | Unsatisfactory |
|---|---|---|---|---|---|
| Works well with others | ☐ | ☐ | ☐ | ☐ | ☐ |
| Reliability | ☐ | ☐ | ☐ | ☐ | ☐ |
| Initiative | ☐ | ☐ | ☐ | ☐ | ☐ |
| Promptness | ☐ | ☐ | ☐ | ☐ | ☐ |
| Conviction | ☐ | ☐ | ☐ | ☐ | ☐ |
| Leadership Ability | ☐ | ☐ | ☐ | ☐ | ☐ |

GENERAL COMMENTS:

_____

_____

_____

*See the "Writing Skills" guidelines for help in evaluating writing skills.

*Employment Issues*

**POTENTIAL:**  Yes  No

Should be considered for promotion
to higher managerial position. (Specify position.)   ☐   ☐

____mos. Estimated number of months until next promotion will be warranted.

Discuss additional skills or development needed before promotion:

_____
_____
_____
_____
_____
_____

GENERAL COMMENTS:

_____
_____
_____

# WRITING SKILLS GUIDELINES

Evaluating an employee's writing skills will be easier if you keep in mind the following characteristics of good written communication:

## WRITING SKILLS CHECKLIST

1) Use of the Five C's
   Is the writing
   clear?

   concise?

   complete?

   considerate?

   comprehensible?

2) Use of persuasive language

3) Style

4) Mechanics

Accompany the evaluation with a covering memo, stating the date of the evaluation and summarizing your conclusions. Keep in mind that this document will become a permanent part of the employee's file, and it merits a great deal of care and thought in writing.

# Chapter 5

# Motivation

## SPECIAL RECOGNITION

Qualities to aim for in letters of congratulation and special recognition are:

- Brevity
- Sincerity
- Enthusiam

These letters can build a bond between individual employees and management. Be on the lookout for occasions such as community service by an employee, professional honors bestowed upon a co-worker, speeches given, etc. Following are a couple of examples of such letters.

### For Civic Service

Dear Fran:

I noted with pleasure the article in last night's paper announcing that you had volunteered to head the March of Dimes fund drive in the Boston metro area. You are always going one step (or more!) beyond what is required, Fran, and this kind of extra effort is what makes you both a special person and a valued member of Acme. All of us are proud of you. Congratulations!

Sincerely,

*Business Writing Made Simple*

## For Professional Honor

Dear Ted:

How pleased and proud I was to hear you have been named "<u>Outstanding Engineer of the Year</u>" <u>by your ASME Chapter</u>! At <u>Acme</u>, we have always known you are an exceptionally talented <u>engineer</u>, and it is gratifying to see such ability receive professional recognition. Congratulations, <u>Ted</u>!

Sincerely,

## To an Employee for a Job Well Done

Dear Tony:

I just wanted to tell you once again what a fine job you did on the <u>Baxter presentation</u> yesterday. Your presentation was professional, personable and highly motivating. After your fine work, I am confident <u>Acme</u> will get the <u>Baxter</u> account.

I know you put a lot of time and effort into the presentation, <u>Tony</u>, and I want to assure you that it showed! Thank you for a job well done.

Sincerely,

# GOODWILL

The same guidelines apply to general letters of goodwill as to those of special recognition: brevity, sincerity and enthusiam. Goodwill is merely an attitude but a most important one. Foster it among employees, customers, vendors, the community and competitors.

## To Employees at Year End

Fellow Employees:

Congratulations and sincere thanks are in order for each of you -- Acme just completed its best sales year ever. All your hard work paid off for Acme and for you. We are pleased to announce an end-of-year-bonus larger than ever before. Look for it in your next pay envelope. It is our way of telling you how much we appreciate your work.

While we know you will be delighted with the bonus, we hope you realize it is simply one way of saying how proud we are of your dedication, enthusiasm and talent. Each of you has contributed not only to a good sales record but, more importantly, to giving Acme the family feeling which has always made it special. Thank you, and may next year bring you more success and happiness.

Sincerely,

## To Customer, Newly Promoted

Dear Ms. Doe:

I just heard of your promotion to Chief Purchasing Agent and wanted to send along my congratulations. I have long been impressed with your professionalism and efficiency and am pleased that it has been duly recognized by your management. Keep up the good work!

Sincerely,

# Chapter 6

# Personal Touches

## ANNOUNCEMENTS

### Birth of First Child

Dear Chris:

Congratulations on the birth of <u>Samantha</u>. We are delighted for you and your <u>wife/husband</u>, and wish you all the best at this turning point in your life together. Please share our congratulations with your <u>wife/husband</u>. We are looking forward to seeing the first pictures!

Sincerely,

### Birth of Subsequent Children

Dear Chris:

We were so pleased to hear about the birth of <u>Jack</u>. You and your <u>wife/husband</u> must be very proud of your growing family, and we share your joy in life renewing itself. We look forward to seeing pictures of the newest <u>Draken (surname)</u>. Please congratulate your <u>wife/husband</u> for us.

Sincerely,

### Adoption

```
Dear Sam and Alice:
We are so pleased to hear of the new member of the Draken
family.  You are to be congratulated and admired for
opening your home and hearts to this child.  He/she
couldn't have a better chance in life than the one you are
giving him/her.  We are proud of you and wish you all the
best.
Sincerely,
```

# ANNOUNCEMENT OF RETIREMENT

## To Employee

As with the letter announcing a retirement to the employees of a company, the letter written from the firm to the retiring individual must be personal, light, and appreciative. Keep these points in mind:

- Show pride in the employee's professional accomplishments and confidence in the future.

- Let retirees know that they will be missed. Include an invitation to drop in and say "hi" or state that you will be keeping in touch from time to time.

```
Dear Tom:
I can't believe that 20 years have slipped by since you
were sitting opposite me in your interview.  What an
outstanding contribution you have made to the growth of
Acme.  Your savvy marketing sense and ability to motivate
employees have no parallel at Acme.  And that's why we are
going to miss you -- but it is also why we know you will
turn your retirement into renewal.

Your many friends at Acme will be expecting you to drop in
from time to time.  We know you put too much into Acme to
want to leave it all behind.  We will keep you posted on
major developments, Tom, and trust you will do likewise.
Best wishes on your new adventures!
Sincerely,
```

*Personal Touches*

## To Company

A retiring employee is at a delicate stage in life, and a retirement announcement should be carefully worded. Be sure it gives credit for a job well done and wishes the retiree well. Keep it brief, respectful but light, and give it a positive tone.

The mood of the letter will depend on the person's position and personality. The following sample letter assumes a well-liked, affable employee. For a less light-hearted person, a more serious tone should be adopted. But whenever possible, infuse a little humor into the letter.

```
Fellow Employees:

At last we know why Ed Jones has been smiling so much
lately -- and what those Bermuda pamphlets were doing on
his desk. Ed is retiring as of April 1 and heading
straight to Bermuda. We will both envy and miss him.

In his 17 years with Acme, Ed has made outstanding
contributions to the company and many good friends. All of
us wish him the best for his new life of leisure. We know
Ed's enthusiam and drive will quickly convert his new found
leisure into solid contributions to his community.

Sincerely,
```

## To Customers

Most likely, the customer will be concerned about who will take over the account when the current representative retires. Therefore, it is important to couple the announcement of retirement with an introduction of the replacing representative. Assure the customer that the new person is experienced, competent and anxious to please. Arrange a meeting between the new representative and the customer, if they do not already know one another and suggest the date in the letter.

```
Dear Ms. Doe:

You are no doubt aware that Ms. Albert, your long-time
contact, will retire from her vice-presidency at Acme
Products on January 1, 1986.

Ms. Albert has been with Acme for 15 years and has garnered
many loyal associates and clients in that time. She has
often mentioned that her association with you has been one
of her most rewarding ones. We know that you will miss
her, but that you also share our feeling that she has
definitely earned the right to her leisure time!

As you would expect of such a fine employee, Ms. Albert has
spent the past year breaking in her replacement, Mr. Jones.
Mr. Jones has been with Acme for 10 years, and is
thoroughly familiar with your account. He is
conscientious, knowledgeable and very likeable person --
```

perfect for your account.  Ms. Albert would like to introduce you to him on her next call, December 15.  We are confident that your association with him will be a long and successful one.

Sincerely,

# INVITATIONS, FORMAL

## Issuing

Formal invitations for official luncheons, dinners or receptions should be engraved. If engraving is not possible, then they should be handwritten on conservative paper. They should be issued about two weeks before the event, unless it is holiday time, when more advance notice would be necessary. The following items are included in an invitation:

- Reason for the occasion.
- Date, time, place.
- Notation of dress, if appropriate.
- R.S.V.P. address/phone.

Sample invitation to a formal luncheon, honoring Board Chairman:

```
              The Board of Directors
         of Acme Products, Incorporated
       requests the pleasure of your company
            at a luncheon in honor of
         Mr. Robert Acme, Chairman of the Board
          Thursday, the twenty-first of March
                 at one o'clock
```

```
R.S.V.P.                              Aboard
Ms. Sarah Brown                       The Sea Wonder
Acme Products, Incorporated           Appleton Marina
21 Main Street
Appleton, Wisconsin 55445
```

## Accepting

Invitations are accepted in as formal a manner as they are extended. Formal invitations call for a handwritten reply in the third person on the first side of the most conservative stationery. Telephoning or telegraphing is also acceptable. It is advisable to repeat the date, place and time, just to avoid misunderstandings.

When replying in writing, follow this format:

> Mr. Franklin Delrow
> accepts with pleasure
> the kind invitation of
> The Board of Directors,
> Acme Products, Incorporated
> for luncheon
> on Thursday, the twenty-first of March
> at one o'clock
> at the Appleton Marina

## Declining

The same rules apply for declining a formal invitation, with the addition of a brief mention as to why the person cannot attend.

> Mr. Franklin Delrow
> regrets
> that due to a previous engagement
> he will be unable to accept the kind invitation of
> The Board of Directors
> of Acme Products, Incorporated
> for the twenty-first of March
> at the Appleton Marina

*Personal Touches*

# INVITATIONS, INFORMAL

## Issuing

Informal invitations may be issued by telephone or in writing. An R.S.V.P. on written invitations is optional—you can omit it entirely, replace it with "Regrets only" or use it as is. Like formal invitations, informal ones are issued two weeks in advance, except at holiday time when up to six weeks is permissible.

When written invitations are issued, they should be on "Informals": fold-over cards printed or engraved with initials, name and address, or simply decorations. They may be in any color, with black or colored ink. On the informal, simply write:

```
              Cocktails Friday
         IMPRINTED NAME OF HOST/HOSTESS
                March 10, 4-6
                                    21 Main Street
                             Appleton, Wisconsin 55445
```

## Accepting

When there is no R.S.V.P. on an informal invitation, the host/hostess assumes you will come if you can, but it is polite to reply even when not requested. When a written invitation is issued, respond in kind, on "informals":

> *We accept with pleasure for cocktails March 6th at four.*
> *(signed)*

## Declining

Regrets are extended at the same level of formality as the invitation. Use stationery comparable to that of the invitation, and similar wording as well.

> *So sorry I can't make it on the 21st - I'll be out of town.*
> *(signed)*

## INVITATIONS, LETTERHEAD

On rare occasions, you may have to issue an invitation (to an exhibit, for instance), on executive stationery (letterhead). In this instance, the letter is written just as a regular business letter, with the exception that the salutation and complimentary close are omitted. For these invitations:

- Open in a cordial manner.
- Give motivation for attendance.
- Include date, time, occasion, directions, etc.
- Encourage attendance—subtly—in the final paragraph.

```
LETTERHEAD
(Executive Stationery)
July 12, 1986
(inside address)
YOU ARE CORDIALLY INVITED:
```

to come to our Trade Fair in the Civic Auditorium, Main Street, Appleton, Wisconsin, from 10 a.m. to 5 p.m. on July 30, 1986.

You will meet all the Acme Products people you deal with as well as see the latest product line designed to meet your industrial needs. We think that you will find the Fair interesting and informative. Those attending always leave with a few ideas to take back to the head office.

(signed)

Ellis Foster, Sales Manager

# CONDOLENCES

Sincerity and tact are the two most important factors in a letter of condolence. Do not philosophize, quote scripture or poetry. Concentrate on comforting the reader. While brevity is generally preferable, longer letters are acceptable if you know the bereaved well. Although letters to friends should be in longhand, condolences to little-known business associates can properly be typed on letterhead. But if in doubt, write the letter in longhand.

## To Business Associate of the Deceased

Dear Mr. Adams:

It was with deep regret that I learned of the sudden passing of <u>Alex Fox</u>. I know that the death of your <u>close friend and business associate</u> of so many years is a deep loss for you.

All of us will miss <u>Alex</u>, for we all admired his integrity, talents and friendliness. I know how close you were to him, and therefore send you my sincere sympathy upon the loss of your <u>friend and trusted associate</u>.

Sincerely,

## To a Widow(er) of an Employee

Dear Mr./Mrs. Fox:

It was with a deep sense of personal loss that I learned today of the death of your <u>husband/wife</u>. <u>Chris</u> and I were friends as well as co-workers for years. <u>He/she</u> was loved and respected by everyone at <u>Acme</u>, and we share your loss.

My heartfelt sympathy goes out to you and your family. Please feel free to call upon me at any time in these next few weeks if there is any way I can be helpful.

Sincerely,

## Upon Personal Injury or Ilness

Dear Alex:

We were so sorry to hear of your <u>accident</u>, but heartened by the reports that you are recovering quickly. We certainly miss you, <u>Alex</u>, and hope you are soon well enough to return to work. Nobody here can really fill your shoes!

May your recovery continue to be a speedy one.

Sincerely,

## FUND RAISING

Most companies have consolidated fund drives, such as the United Fund, which make one annual appeal. One of the most successful ways to conduct a high-percentage contribution drive is to link the contribution to a personal benefit for the employee. The following letter takes advantage of that fact and offers two benefits to the employee.

## WHEN YOU GIVE—YOU GET

It is time for the annual <u>United Fund</u> drive at <u>Acme</u>. You already know the good feeling you get by helping those less fortunate than you by contributing your Fair Share (<u>0.5</u>% of your annual salary), but this year you stand to gain more than a feeling...

        GIVE YOUR FAIR SHARE:

        GET A DAY OFF and

A CHANCE TO WIN ANOTHER WEEK OFF!

Yes, you will automatically receive a day off during the next 12 months -- when you want it -- just for "doing the right thing": sharing your good fortune with others. What's more, there will be a drawing for Fair Share donors after the drive, and the winner will get an additional week of paid vacation this year. It is Acme's way of rewarding you for your generosity.

So sign your pledge card today. When you give, you get!

# Chapter 7

# Administration

## ACKNOWLEDGING LETTERS RECEIVED IN CO-WORKER'S ABSENCE

There will be times when correspondence arrives for one of your co-workers or managers who is away on vacation or business. If it will be some time before the addressee returns, business etiquette calls for an acknowledgment of the letter. When you write such a letter, here are three things to include:

- State that the person is away from the office and the date on which he will return. (Unless the person who wrote the letter knows the absent person or the situation well, it is not necessary to explain the absence.)
- Give the writer an assurance that the letter will be brought to the absent person's attention upon his return.
- Should the delay in response cause any inconvenience, a note of apology can be added.

```
Dear Mr. Doe:

Ms. Adams is out of the office, and will not return until
August 10.  Therefore, I am acknowledging your letter of
July 15 regarding the installation of new copiers.

As soon as Ms. Adams returns, I will be sure that she sees
your letter.  No doubt she will be in touch with you
shortly after her return.

Sincerely,
```

*Business Writing Made Simple*

Should you wish to go beyond a simple acknowledgment and actually respond to the subject matter in the letter, be sure to explain the surrounding situation so that no misunderstanding ensues.

The steps for responding to a letter are:

- State that the person written to is away and give the expected date of return.

- Identify your function, if the writer would not otherwise know you.

- Respond to the writer's query, briefly restating his facts (or citing the letter) and telling him just what you can do for him. Be specific and be very clear, especially if you are committing the absent person to do something or stating his position.

- When appropriate, tell the writer that the absent person will respond upon his return.

```
Dear Mr. Doe:

Ms. Adams will be out of town until August 10.  As her
administrative assistant, I will be pleased to handle the
details regarding installation of the new copiers which you
mentioned in your letter of July 15.  Would August 1 at 10
a.m. in my office be convenient for the meeting you
requested?

Sincerely,
```

*Administration*

## CONFIRMATIONS

This ranks among the easiest of letters/memos to write, as all you must do is confirm in writing a request that is being granted.

To confirm something:

- State exactly what the request was and that it is being granted.
- State who will be granting the request.
- Tell the person when he can expect the request to be granted.
- To foster goodwill, add that you are glad to be able to help the person/firm by granting the request.

Dear Mr. Tunny:

Thank you for requesting that <u>Mr. Dean</u>, <u>the Chairman of the Board of</u> <u>Acme Products</u>, Inc., address your <u>Rotary Club luncheon meeting</u> on <u>December 4</u>. He is delighted to accept the invitation and is looking forward to it.

<u>Acme Products</u> is pleased to support the fine work of the <u>Rotary Club</u>.

Sincerely,

# AUTHORIZATIONS

When you are requesting work that entails a considerable amount of time or money, a letter of authorization is recommended. It can serve a number of purposes: clearly defining the direction, scope, and purpose of the work; setting the budget limit (when appropriate); and serving as a guideline for evaluating whether the completed project meets all the requirements. Formal reports frequently contain a copy of the letter of authorization.

A letter of authorization should include:

- A detailed description of the project, along with any restrictions or requirements.
- The due date.
- The name of the person who is responsible for the project.
- Budgetary limit, when appropriate.
- Name of the person to whom the project/report is to be delivered.

```
Dear Ms. Doe:

This authorizes you to conduct an employee attitude survey
at Acme Products.  The areas surveyed should include: (1)
employee morale; (2) satisfaction about benefit packages;
(3) interest in flexi-time and (4) suggested improvements.
[Discussion of questionnaire construction, etc., goes
here.]

The questionnaire should be ready for my approval on
October 1, 1985, and the interviewing should be completed
by October 31.  The final report should reach me by
November 15.

We hope that your survey will be another step in our effort
to make sure that Acme employees are happy with their jobs.
Please let me know if you have any questions about the
survey.

Sincerely,
```

## INITIATING WORK

Usually an interoffice work request will be sent on memo stationery. There is little difference between a letter of authorization and a memo initiating work. The latter is just a bit more informal, and should include:

- A description of the work being requested. Clarity is of the utmost importance here. It will help avoid misunderstandings and ensure that you get what you are looking for. It can also be useful in evaluating the work, serving as a checklist of requirements.

- Deadlines.

- Any information that will be necessary for the person to complete the work.

- An offer to discuss the project if help or advice is needed.

- The name of the person who is to receive the work, if other than the person requesting it.

```
DATE: November 10, 1985
TO: Ms. Doe
FROM: Mr. Smith
RE: Budget for First Quarter, 1986
```

Please prepare a budget summary on your account, X-O Soap, for the First Quarter of 1986. Include production, media and research costs, broken down by month.

I would like the budget by November 15. Please call if you have any questions.

(signed) Mr. Smith

# LETTERS OF TRANSMITTAL

A letter of transmittal accompanies reports to a sponsor or organization. Written by the author of the report, it is like a preface. It states that the report is being delivered, and refers to the authorization for the report. It follows the format of a regular business letter, and is signed by the author. One page is usually sufficient.

Here is a list of the mandatory and optional data in a letter of transmittal:

**Mandatory:**

- Notation of transmittal and authorization.
- Brief statement of the topic of the report or explanation of the job requested.
- Statement of appreciation and offer of future help.

**Optional:**

- Summary of results.
- Acknowledgment of special help.
- Description of the report format, if unusual.
- Miscellaneous facts not included in the report but which may be of interest to the reader.
- Listing of conclusions and recommendations.
- Explanation of data gathering/generating methods.
- Mention of limitations or problems. This should be stated in a positive tone, so it doesn't end up sounding like an apology.

```
Dear Ms. Doe:

Here is the Employee Attitude Survey and Analysis which you
authorized me to conduct in your letter of September 15,
1986. You asked that the survey cover (1) employee morale,
(2) satisfaction about benefit packages, (3) interest in
flexi-time and (4) suggested improvements.

I have concluded that the employees of Acme Products are
generally quite satisfied with their jobs and benefits, and
that flexi-time would increase their job satisfaction.

I hope that the report will be of use to you and your
department in your continuing effort to improve employee
morale. Please let me know if I can be of further
assistance.

Sincerely,
```

# REQUESTING INFORMATION

This is one of the letters you will write most frequently. Fortunately, you can keep these letters very brief and to the point.

You should:

- State clearly but briefly the information you are seeking.

- Include a date for the response, rather than the standard "at your earliest convenience" or "as soon as possible."

- Explain the reason for your request only when courtesy demands it—or when you think the request may not be granted otherwise. You should also explain the request if you think it would clarify the nature of the information you are seeking. By giving the reader an idea of your goal, you may help him help you.

- Be sure to thank the recipient for his effort.

```
Dear Ms. Doe:
Please send me a copy of your latest pamphlet, "Investing
in Your Future."  I would appreciate receiving this by
November 15, if possible.
Please send the pamphlet to:
     name
     address
Thank you for your cooperation.
Sincerely,
```

## REQUESTING RESERVATIONS

Short and simple does it for these letters. Just include:

- Name(s) for whom the reservation is being made.
- Date and approximate time of arrival. Be sure to note a late arrival, when appropriate, so the reservation will be held. Guarantee the reservation if required.
- Period during which the hotel, car, or service will be required.
- A description of the room(s), car, or services being booked. Note any special facilities needed.
- A request for confirmation. (Give name and address if not obvious from the letterhead.)

Dear Mr. Jackson:

Please reserve a suite of rooms (living room, bedroom with private bath, and reception room) for March 10 through 15, 1985 (six nights) for Ms. Jones of Acme Products. She will be arriving late the evening of the 15th.

Please send me a written confirmation of these arrangements.

Sincerely,

## REQUESTING A SPEAKER

The best way to get a speaker to accept your invitation is to point out the mutual benefits. Point out that not only will your company benefit, but the speaker also will be getting something in return—money, recognition, contacts, or simply an opportunity to express ideas.

Other points to cover in such a letter are:

- Gratitude (in advance) for accepting the engagement.
- The topic for the speech. Give reasons for the request, if appropriate.
- Type of audience.
- Date, place, and time of the speech; giving an approximate length for the speech may be helpful to the speaker.
- Financial arrangements: payment for the speech (if any).
- Whether travel and accommodations will be paid for by the company.
- Whether the media have been invited to cover the speech.

Dear Mr. Jones:

In this election year, you are no doubt looking for ways to reach your constituents in an efficient, effective manner. We think that the Annual Meeting of Acme Products, a major economic force in your district, would be an excellent place for you to communicate your views. Better yet, you will be able to face your opponent in the mayoral race, Mr. Dimbs, and debate the issues. He has agreed to the debate, and we certainly hope that you will, too.

The meeting will be held October 8, at 2 p.m. in the Ballroom of the Grand Hotel, 112 Main Street. All local broadcast stations have been invited to cover the 30-minute debate.

We would be very grateful if you would accept this challenge, Mr. Jones, and hope to hear from you shortly. Thank you!

Sincerely,

# MINUTES

The preparation of complete minutes starts with accurate, clear notes taken during the meeting. Another key to writing good minutes is to do it as soon as you can after the meeting. Gaps in notes will be filled in by your memory if you write them immediately. (If you do not attend the meeting, make sure you get to the person responsible for giving you the information immediately.)

Some firms have special books and stationery for recording minutes. If so, be sure to do a draft and get it approved before entering it in the book. Short of any corporate format for minutes, do the following:

- Name the group, and list the names of those who attended the meeting, specifiying the chairperson.
- Record the time, place, and date of the meeting.
- List the topics discussed in headings for ease of reference.
- Put the points covered underneath each heading. Be objective.
- Record decisions made, noting any assignments and due dates.
- Identify yourself as the preparer of the minutes.
- Have another person who attended the meeting review your minutes before they are distributed.

```
                    Acme Products, Inc.
                   Department Heads' Meeting
Minutes of the Department Heads' Meeting, November 10,
1985
Chairperson Ames called the meeting to order at 9:30 a.m.
in the Conference Room of the Acme Products Administration
Building.  Attending were:  T. Ames, S. Jones, R. Pearson,
C. Reardon.  The minutes of the October 10 meeting were
accepted.
     REPORTS:
     Employee Attitude Survey
Mr. Smith reported on the results of the recently
conducted employee attitude survey.  He indicated that
overall employee satisfaction was at a  high level and
that the adoption of flexi-time may further increase
satisfaction.
     Research
```

*Administration*

Ms. Jones of the Research Department presented findings and conclusions of the newly issued Consumer Study. (Summary of her report goes here.)

    ANNOUNCEMENTS:

    Budgets

The Chairperson called for submission of 1986 budgets by the next Department Heads' meeting, <u>December 4.</u>

The meeting was adjourned at <u>11 a.m.</u>

                                    Respectfully submitted,

                                      (signature and title)

# Section III

# Writing Effective Management Reports

# Chapter 8

# Five Steps to Effective Reports

The key to writing an effective report is to keep in mind that the purpose is to *communicate* something to the *reader*. By following the guidelines for good communication covered in Section I, you can avoid report writers' most common mistakes: trying to impress rather than communicate; rambling rather than being concise and organized; and writing above or below the reader's level of familiarity/expertise rather than gearing the information to the audience.

Let's take a closer look at each of the key elements: communication and reader.

## Communication

Too many writers see a report as an opportunity to show off. You've seen the results—long words used where simple ones would have sufficed, technical terms that are beyond the audience's grasp, and a pompous, laborious tone. This not only makes for poor communication, but also reflects poorly on the author. Instead of impressing management, a report like this simply convinces readers that the author is conceited—and is a poor communicator, too. Remember that the best communication is simple and direct. Whenever possible, simplify for clarity and impact.

A report that rambles is counterproductive for two reasons: 1) It annoys readers who would rather spend their time doing something other than wading through your prose; 2) It confuses readers who lose sight of your real purpose. Rambling reports are usually the result of inadequate planning. A complete, well-organized outline will save you time and improve the finished product. Later in this chapter you will learn how to plan your report with the help of just such an outline.

### Reader

Keeping the reader in mind as you prepare your report will assure maximum impact. If your writing is not targeted to your audience, they will fail to get your message and will not be motivated to act as you wish. Write the report as if you were talking to one person—always keeping the expertise, interest and viewpoint of the reader in mind. This will maximize your influence because you are addressing yourself to the concerns of the reader. Obviously this will be easier when the report is being written for a specific individual; but even when it is going to a group, design it to suit the group's needs and wants.

## HOW TO USE THIS SECTION

This section presents the practical five-step guide to writing effective management reports. It will take you from the planning stage to the presentation of the final report. Following these guidelines will assure a professional, letter-perfect report which will impress top management and reflect favorably on you.

This chapter, Five Steps to Effective Reports, covers in detail the planning, writing and editing of a full-dress report. It follows the general guidelines for basic effective business writing given in the first section of this book plus gives you the detailed information you need to know when writing a full-dress report.

If you are writing a less formal document, simply pick and choose among the sections to put together a report suiting your taste and task. The guidelines and formats offered in here are appropriate for a wide range of management reports.

The next chapter deals with specific types of management reports, giving guidelines and formats for each. Included are: departmental status and research reports; progress reports; research study summaries, and management recommendations. This section concentrates on how to be thorough, impactful and persuasive in getting your points across.

### The Five-step System

The five steps to writing impressive reports are as follows.

**1. Plan.** Before any writing can begin, you must *plan*. Use the process spelled out here to plan your report. Define your objective; gather the information you need; analyze the information; and form your conclusions.

**2. Determine the format.** Follow one of the model formats presented in this chapter to organize your information into easy-to-follow arrangement. These models contain the categories that most reports have in common. Use the model as is by inserting your information or use it as a starting point, adapting it to your own needs.

**3. Outline.** Take the time to organize your information into manageable sections in a logical order. You'll see how your job is aided by this organizing and prioritizing step.

**4. Write.** After all the preparatory work is complete, the actual writing of the report will seem easy. You know what you want to say and how you want to say it so the actual writing will go smoothly and quickly.

**5. Edit.** The final step is the polishing that gives your report its professional appearance and ensures that your report's integrity is not jeopardized by simple lack of attention to detail. Check every fact; check grammar and punctuation; check the format; and of course, check for completeness. Your report will be held in higher regard if you pay close attention to this step.

## STEP 1: PLAN THE REPORT

A famous statesman is supposed to have said that if he had only 15 minutes to solve the most difficult problem in the world, he would spend the first twelve of those minutes *planning*—and only three resolving the problem. The same is true in writing. The first step in producing a good report is to plan it carefully and completely before you start writing. Planning also saves time because a well-thought-out scheme will make the actual writing faster and easier. It eliminates surprises and digressions that may call for time-consuming rewrites.

Here are the planning stages:

### Define the Objective

Determine the aim or purpose of the report. Are you trying to inform, to persuade, or both? This decision will influence your organization and mode of presentation, as well as the overall tone of the report.

Consider the subject of the report. How deeply should you go into it? What aspects will be covered?

### Gather the Information

Gather your data in a systematic manner. Make lists of all possible sources of information. Give each source the attention it deserves, and then—as your ideas begin to jell—make lists of the items which should be included in the final report.

Make sure you have included enough information to enable the report to stand on its own. If there is background information not immediately relevant to the report but important to its understanding, plan to cite references or summarize it.

### Analyze the Information

Sort through the material you've gathered. Eliminate irrelevant data, and begin to think about how the remaining information should be organized for effective presentation.

Decide which information is of primary, and which of secondary, importance. Then you can decide what should go into the report itself and what should be included as an appendix. (Basic facts and trends appear in the body of the report, while supporting details, complete in themselves [like statistics or a series of test results], belong in the appendix.)

**Form the Conclusions**

Many people waste a lot of time by beginning to write before they know what they're going to say, hoping that their conclusions will surface as they proceed. Why is it so important to think through your conclusions before you put them in writing? There are two reasons: 1) it saves you the effort of producing endless drafts; and 2) it avoids jumbled, rambling reports.

To form your conclusions before you begin to write, sift through your material and decide what it reveals or indicates. A particular viewpoint will usually emerge after careful analysis. Occasionally, the findings will be too ambiguous to permit any definite conclusion. When this happens, the conclusion then becomes, "The results were inconclusive." If such is the case, you should advocate undertaking new studies or entirely abandoning the line of thinking.

The conclusions must be clear, concise and definite because many report readers focus on the conclusions, giving far less attention to how they were developed in the body of the report.

Guard against "tunnel vision." This is what happens when you assume that your readers will accept your conclusions and/or recommendations because they are self-evident. It's only natural that you will begin to believe your conclusions, but don't make the mistake of thinking that your readers will find them equally convincing. They probably haven't thought about the issue as much as you have, nor do they have the benefit of your research. And there is always the possibility that they may be predisposed to disagree with your proposals. It's up to you to convince them of the merits of your position, and you'll never be able to do so unless you give them the facts.

To avoid "tunnel vision," review your writing with two things in mind. First, make sure you're not just listing results, findings, or facts. You have to supply not just a conclusion but the reasoning behind it as well. If you don't, you may leave your readers with the feeling that "something is missing." There's no guarantee that they'll be able to make the same logical connections that you've made.

The second pitfall is just the opposite: all conclusion and no facts. To avoid this, review your writing to make sure you are not just presenting arguments. Ask yourself, are there enough facts so that your readers can follow your logic while looking at actual data? If you think you might bore your readers (or even insult their intelligence) you can always include the information in an appendix.

## STEP 2: DETERMINE THE FORMAT

Format refers to the shape, size, or general layout of the report. Many companies have adopted standardized formats. This has two advantages: First, it minimizes reader confusion because employees become used to the format and learn where to look for what; and secondly, it makes it easier for writers: they don't have to worry about designing their own format. They can simply take out the "model" and fill in the blanks.

If your company does not have a standardized procedure, or if you are trying to devise one, consider either of the two following forms of organization:

**Type I**:
Summary
Introduction
Findings
Conclusions and/or Recommendations
Appendix

The Type I format mirrors the report's actual development. Findings are presented and analyzed before conclusions are drawn. This type of organization is useful when you think that your conclusions and/or recommendations demand a careful setup—for example, when conclusions are controversial, or not immediately evident or understandable without some background.

**Type II**:
Background
Conclusions and/or Recommendations
Summary of Findings
Detailed Findings
Summary
Appendix

The second format (Type II) is usually more appropriate for management reports (unless the situation dictates the use of the first format as mentioned above). The Type II format is preferable because it highlights the crux of the report—conclusions and recommendations—thus (1) saving time for the reader by putting the "meat" of the report up front, and (2) tuning in the reader to the writer's viewpoint early, facilitating the reader's understanding and interpretation of the findings.

To help you select the proper format, here is a definition of what comprises each of the sections in the two most commonly used report formats:

## Report Type I:

> Summary
> Introduction
> Findings
> Conclusions and/or Recommendations
> Appendix

**Summary.** The summary covers the entire scope of the report, presenting the key findings, conclusions and/or recommendations in a concise manner. A good summary should answer the following questions: Why was the study conducted? What was done? What were the results (findings)? What do the results mean? What should be done about them? In a Type I format, the summary is the first page of the report, giving a busy reader an overall view of the report at a glance.

**Introduction.** The purpose of this section is to orient the reader by providing all the relevant background, such as the purpose of and need for the report, the methods used and specific aspects of the topic covered. After reading this, the reader should be able to understand the content of the report.

**Findings.** This section lists the results of the study or test. In deciding what goes here, rather than in the appendix, use the following criterion: the findings should include all the information readers who are not specialists in the subject need to understand the report. The appendix material is for specialists who want more detailed information and for recordkeeping purposes.

**Conclusions.** The purpose of the conclusions is to interpret the findings. They should also indicate whether the report achieved what it set out to prove or discover. Each conclusion should be followed by a brief supporting statement, recapping the findings which led to drawing that conclusion. However, in reports of a very general (nontechnical or detailed) nature, supporting statements may be omitted.

Conclusions are listed separately, preceded by numbers. Frequently the order of presentation is determined by importance, building from least to most important or vice versa. Other times they may be listed by logical development, time sequence, persuasiveness, etc.

**Recommendations.** Recommendations are the author's advice based on the data generated by the study. They should develop logically from the conclusions, making the recommendations more understandable and convincing to the reader. They are the most important part of the report because they advocate action based on the results of the study.

Recommendations are intended to help the reader use the report, and should be phrased in a clear, tactful manner. Take care to avoid an overly authoritative or dictatorial tone, which could alienate readers.

**Appendix.** Information which is important to the understanding of the report but is too detailed or cumbersome to be incorporated in the body should be presented in the appendix. When there are several distinct topics, put each in a separate appendix. Appendices should be titled and listed separately in the table of contents.

### Report Type II:

>Background
>Conclusions
>Recommendations
>Summary of Findings
>Detailed Findings
>Summary
>Appendix

In this format, the "Background" covers exactly what is in the "Introduction" of a Type I report. The conclusions, recommendations, summary and appendices also contain the same material as in a Type I report. The points of difference lie in the "summary of findings" and "detailed findings."

**Summary of Findings.** Use a summary when a report's findings are so extensive or complex that the reader's understanding may suffer if they are presented *en masse*. Single out the most important findings, or abstract the essence of each, and include them in this section. It will not only clarify your report, but also will save the reader time.

List the findings numerically, with the order being determined by importance, chronology, logic or persuasiveness.

**Detailed Findings.** Expand on each of the summarized findings in this section. Remember to use the appendix for anything too cumbersome or technical for this section. Presenting detailed findings does not mean that you should include anything in the body of the report that would normally belong in an appendix.

## STEP 3: OUTLINE

Now is the time to make an outline. Some people turn this into an unnecessarily difficult task. The most common mistake is trying to make the outline too formal or professional-looking. When the result doesn't measure up, they get discouraged. In most cases, the outline needn't be a formal document. The best approach is to make a list of the items that will be covered in the report, along with a brief summary of what will be said under each heading. This is all you need to give your writing focus and organization.

Following is a sample of the outline used to prepare the report presented at the end of this chapter.

# Sample Outline for Type I Report

Recommendation on Acme Soap Package Copy

SUMMARY

The best descriptive phrase to use is "The Finnish Fresh Soap."

    Methods used to detemine this:
1. Positioning study
2. Alternatives
3. Evaluation of industry standards
4. Expert opinion
5. FTC/FCC concerns

INTRODUCTION

    ABC Agency was requested by Acme Soap to determine most effective phrase.

    The Agency is confident all issues have been considered.

    The phrase has appeared in advertising but not on the package.

    Test commercials are ready for copy testing.

    Marketing plan is ready for presentation to management pending resolution of legal issue.

FINDINGS

    Positioning study reveals positive sales impact.

    Alternatives are not as effective.

    Phrase uniquely positions Acme Soap.

    Experts like it.

    Continuity should be maintained.

    Phrase does not violate FTC/FCC regulations.

RECOMMENDATION

The agency recommends that the current phrase be maintained and the concept be presented to management.

*Business Writing Made Simple*

Now that you have finished planning, formatting, and outlining the report, it is time for Step Four: Writing the Report.

## STEP 4: WRITE THE REPORT

The first three steps have prepared you for this stage of the process—writing. Careful preparation makes the writing task easier. Writing requires some solitude for best results. You'll write more quickly and effectively if you can maintain your concentration. It is nearly impossible to compose an organized document in the midst of daily office activity. Escape to the library or conference room or, if this is impossible, consider writing it before or after regular business hours.

Take the outline you've written and divide it into sections. Work on expanding each section of the outline one at a time. This will overcome the "hugeness" of the task. The idea of writing one section is less discouraging than thinking of the report as a whole. It will also ensure that you will concentrate on the important details of each section that might have eluded you if you were trying to write the whole project at once.

When writing each section of the rough draft, the important thing is to get everything down on paper. Don't fret over phrasing—just organize your data and get it on the page. You can sort it out and work on sentence structure, transitions, persuasive techniques, and other refinements later.

If you communicate best verbally, take advantage of this talent by dictating your rough draft; if you are more at home with a pencil and reams of paper, write it out. The point is to make the task as easy for yourself as possible, and to maximize the report's effectiveness by using your best means of communication.

You may write the sections in the order they will appear in the report, or write them out of sequence—whatever makes sense for your particular task. However, be sure to write the summary last, no matter where it appears in the report.

A good summary can only be developed after the body of the report has been written. If you try to write the summary first, you will probably have to redo it later to incorporate unexpected angles or viewpoints which developed during the report writing.

### Report Contents

No matter which format you use, the report should incorporate some, if not all, of the design features listed below. The list covers all the items required in a full-dress report, so just omit those sections that do not apply to your particular task. The notes accompanying each section will guide you in producing a professional, well-written report.

**Cover page.** The cover page protects the letter of authorization and identifies the title, subject and author of the report. Do not number this as the pagination of a report begins with the title page.

**Letter of authorization.** You may insert a copy of the letter that assigned you the task of conducting the study or preparing the report. (An example of such a letter and discussion of the contents appears in Section II of this book.) When placed before the title page, it is not numbered.

**Title page.** This first page of the report supplies the title, names and job titles of the report's sponsor and author, and the place and date of writing.

Keep the title of the report as simple and as short as possible.

Each segment of information on the title page should be centered horizontally and well spaced vertically. Present this information in the order given above, with vertical space between items—except the place and date, which can be placed one below the other at the bottom of the page.

**Letter of transmittal.** (See Section II for a sample of this letter.) In addition to the information given in Section II, a transmittal letter may also contain:

- A brief summary of the results or findings;
- Acknowledgements of special help;
- An explanation of the report's format or organization, if it is unusual;
- Interesting sidelights to the study which may be informative to the reader;
- Mention of any unusual experiences you had in preparing the report which do not appear in the text;
- Announcement of conclusions and recommendations, with major supporting reasons (include this only when you are not using a "conclusions last" format);
- A summary of procedures or methods;
- Mention of limitations or problems accompanying the report—but be sure to avoid an apologetic tone.

When deciding which of the above items to include, keep in mind that the letter should be no more than one page long, yet it must contain everything the reader needs to understand the report. As you write the letter of transmittal, think of what you would tell someone in person when handing him the report.

The letter should look like a regular business letter, with a salutation, complimentary close, signature, etc. It is counted as page ii of the report (after the title page), but the number is usually omitted since it would look out of place on a letter.

**Table of contents.** This is the "roadmap" of the report in that it tells the reader what is in the report and where to find it. Naturally, it is only necessary for long reports. It looks and functions like an outline of the report and for this reason should be written only after you have completed the rough draft.

What to include:

- Letters of transmittal. If including this crowds the contents page or makes it run to two pages consider excluding it.
- All the major headings of the report (placed at the left margin, with secondary headings indented underneath).
- The bibliography.
- The appendices. These are usually referred to by title, not by the word "appendix." They are numbered consecutively after the text.

The table of contents is the first page to be numbered. (Remember that preceding pages have been placed in a particular order, but page numbers are not placed on them.) Center the number at the bottom of the contents page, and center the title ("Contents" or "Table of Contents") at the top.

You should take considerable care in putting the table of contents together. The language should be **descriptive** and yet easily understood by the reader. The format should make the relative importance of the various sections obvious. This is often done by showing major topics in capital letters (or underscored) and secondary topics with only the first letter capitalzed. Ideally, the reader should be able to grasp the logic and overall flow of your report simply by skimming the table of contents.

**List of tables, charts and illustrations.** If you have over five pieces of illustrative data (or charts and tables), you may want to list them under a special heading, following the table of contents.

**Visuals.** When writing the report, determine whether to use visuals by asking yourself these questions:

- Will the chart or table help the reader to understand particularly complex data?
- Will a chart or table save the reader time?
- Will a chart or table conveniently collect information for easy reference?

Charts and tables fall into two groups: Illustrative visuals, which are used to amplify or clarify a point; and collective visuals, which compile data in an orderly fashion. The latter, along with very lengthy visuals, are usually placed in the appendix. This avoids awkward breaks in the text of the report. Summarize long visuals in smaller charts, tables, and graphs when inserting them in the text, and be sure to place them near the relevant subject matter. In addition, consider the following guidelines:

- Don't use tables as a substitute for textual analysis; use them to supplement or emphasize it.
- If the text makes the point very clear, consider omitting a planned table—it may not be necessary.
- When using a visual, include introductory and concluding references to it in the text.

- A good table or chart allows the reader to skim the text, study the chart and get the point.
- Make the chart or graph's title meaningful and specific, with a caption that further clarifies its purpose.
- The layout of the chart should be visually uncomplicated; the chart should illustrate only one point; and components should be clearly and concisely labeled.

See Appendix V, Tables and Graphs in Reports, for more information on preparing effective visuals.

## Making Your Report Better

Here are some hints for the important segments of information included in your report.

**Background:** Think of this section as the foundation on which the rest of the report relies. Do your best to make a good impression. Be specific and factual in your description of how, why, when, and where your data was collected. Concentrate on convincing your readers that your data and judgment are reliable.

Just as it is usually better to write the summary last (in order to make sure it accurately reflects the report), you probably will find that you have to rework the background section after the rough draft of the entire report is completed. The task of writing the report may lead to new discoveries or ways of looking at things, and the background must often be revised to reflect these changes. Remember that the background section is one of the first things most readers will see. Think of it as a promise of things to come, and make sure that the body of the report will deliver all that had been promised.

**Conclusions:** Your conclusions should follow logically from the findings presented in the report. But no matter how sound your reasoning, the agreement and support you are able to elicit from your reader depend on how your conclusions are presented.

Language is a prime consideration here. Don't let your own enthusiasm carry you beyond the limits of moderation and reasonableness. You shouldn't have to overstate your case to get your reader's support—nor will adopting a strident tone guarantee his agreement. In fact, language that is unnecessarily harsh can actually turn your reader against you. It is far better to aim for a straightforward but moderate expression of your conclusions. It is better to say, for example, that "Acme's Riverton is unprofitable" than to say "Acme's Riverton plant is bleeding corporate profits." You don't have to be vague or indecisive—just reasonable. If your conclusions are backed up by verifiable facts, logic, expert opinions, illustrations, analogies, and other indisputable forms of support, you shouldn't have to rely on verbal fireworks.

There will be times when conclusions will emerge that do not agree with your recommendations. Don't undermine your report's integrity by omitting them. If your format calls for presenting the conclusions first, you may want to give a little more background or explanation, since the reader will not have had the benefit of the body of the report which leads up to them.

When it comes to determining the order in which the conclusions themselves will be presented, let logic be your guide. Here are four suggested approaches:

    1. Most significant or persuasive first; least significant or persuasive last.

    2. Positive conclusions first; negative ones last.

    3. The order in which the subjects were presented in the report.

    4. The order dictated by inductive or deductive reasoning.

Sometimes it is difficult to differentiate between conclusions and recommendations. In deciding which is which, ask yourself "what is the situation?" (conclusion) and "what should be done about it?" (recommendation).

**Recommendations:** Recommendations should be clearly based on the conclusions, and should be appropriate to the situation—that is, affordable and feasible. But it is equally important to stand by your convictions and recommend what you feel is necessary or justified. There is often a temptation to avoid "rocking the boat" by trying to design recommendations that won't offend anyone—but it should be resisted. If you have done your job well in preparing the report, it will validate even what appears to be an unpopular recommendation.

Language plays an important role in stating the recommendations as well as the conclusions. Strive for a tone that suggests rather than commands; be to the point, but not curt. After all, this is the heart of the report, the part that carries the most weight and demands the most attention. It's worth making sure that your efforts aren't undermined by a poor choice of words.

**Bibliography:** A bibliography is a listing of all your sources, including interviews, articles, books, and research reports. It serves a dual purpose: (1) It shows your readers that you have done your homework; and (2) It allows them to double-check your sources and do further research on their own.

You should list all sources that you cite or quote. The order in which you list them is a matter of preference. Alphabetical, order-of-appearance, or order-of-importance arrangements are all acceptable, but whatever method you use, make sure that you explain the system to the reader. (A guide to bibliograpies can be found in Appendix IV.)

Pages of a bibliography are numbered consecutively continuing the text numbers.

**Appendix:** By using an appendix, you can avoid cluttering up your writing with information that is important, but that might be distracting if included in the main body of the report. An appendix is the place for information that the reader will need to confirm, validate, or follow up on your conclusions, data, or recommendations—for example, the sample questionnaire or tabulated data from a survey. Remember that this section is designed to help the reader, so don't fill it with information that will confuse him. And never include anything in an appendix which has not been mentioned in the text. It will be "buried," unless you alert your reader to its existence.

Each item in the appendix should be titled and presented separately in its own section. Sometimes appendices are referred to as exhibits, such as "Exhibit I: Long-range Market Trends." This makes it easier to refer to the supplementary information. The citation in the text would simply say: (See Exhibit I.).

Items in the appendix should be organized according to the order in which they appear in the text. This makes it easier for readers to find this additional data and helps you check to make sure you have not included information in the appendix without first introducing it in the text.

Pages of the appendix are numbered consecutively, continuing the text (or bibliography) numbers. (If the last page of the text or bibliography is 35, the first page of the appended material is 36.)

## STEP 5: EDIT

Now that the bulk of your work is behind you, all that is left is the editing and polishing. This can take some time and effort, but it's always worth it. Just as in any endeavor, the "final touches"—though time-consuming—will give you professional results. Here are some guidelines to follow:

- Make sure you haven't left anything out before you begin editing. (Review notes or old drafts.)
- Place paragraphs in logical sequence: make sure that the entire report flows easily.
- Go through the draft, reading each sentence critically to make sure that it is necessary, correct, sensible, clear, and logical. Don't be afraid to cut and/or clarify. Remember that a report's merit rests on solid ideas, well presented—not the number of pages.
- At this point, you have revised sections which should be quite well written. Now turn to the report as a whole and read it for continuity.
- If possible, let someone else read this draft to get a fresh viewpoint.
- Check for proper grammar and spelling.

Once you have a revised draft which meets the above requirements, review it once again, asking yourself these questions:

|  | Yes | No |
|---|---|---|
| 1. Is it inviting and readable? | ☐ | ☐ |
| 2. Is it organized around a central idea? | ☐ | ☐ |
| 3. Is it clear what you want the reader to do after reading the report? | ☐ | ☐ |
| 4. Is the tone consistent? Is it serious, objective and responsible? | ☐ | ☐ |

5. Is the report logically organized so there are no surprises in the conclusions or recommendations? ☐ ☐
6. Is each point well developed and supported? ☐ ☐
7. Are the grammar and spelling correct? If in doubt, use the dictionary or ask someone else. Don't be embarrassed or shy. Remember, it will be a lot more embarrassing to have uncorrected grammar or spelling appear in a permanent, widely-circulated record. ☐ ☐
8. Is the wording concise and precise? ☐ ☐
9. Is the title appropriate? Does it identify the report's contents and reveal the central idea? ☐ ☐
10. Are there helpful headings and subheadings to guide the reader through the report and emphasize the major points? ☐ ☐
11. Is the report as concise as clarity and completeness permit? ☐ ☐
12. Has the final report been carefully proofread and corrected? ☐ ☐

When you are able to answer *yes* to each of the above questions, you may pat yourself on the back and wait for similar kudos from your readers.

A sample report follows; it is short but illustrates the main points discussed above.

*Sample Report*

**Sample Type I Report**

**Package Copy for Acme Soap**

Recommendations
submitted by
ABC Advertising Agency

```
Package Copy for Acme Soap
       prepared by
        John Mills



       submitted to
        Joseph Jones
       Acme Soap Co.




                              ABC Advertising Agency
                                    March 1, 1985
```

*Sample Report*

(ABC Letterhead)

March 1, 1985

Joseph Jones
Acme Soap Company
45 Elm Street
Fairport, IA

Dear Mr. Jones:

    Here are the results of the study conducted to determine the best phrase to use on Acme Soap packages which you authorized ABC Agency to conduct in your letter of December 20, 1984. You asked that the study cover review of past studies, alternatives, a Positioning Study, expert opinion and examination of FTC/FCC guidelines.

    I have concluded that the current Acme package copy be maintained.

    I hope that the report will be of use to you in your effort to bring about a successful ad campaign. Please let me know if I can be of further assistance.

Sincerely yours,

Table of Contents

```
Letter of Transmittal . . . . . . . . . . . . . . . . . . .i
Summary . . . . . . . . . . . . . . . . . . . . . . . . . 1
Introduction . . . . . . . . . . . . . . . . . . . . . . . 1
Findings . . . . . . . . . . . . . . . . . . . . . . . . . 2
Recommendation . . . . . . . . . . . . . . . . . . . . . . 3
Appendix* . . . . . . . . . . . . . . . . . . . . . . . . 4
```

*Due to space limitations the appendix is not included in this sample report.

Package Copy for Acme Soap

SUMMARY

The ABC Agency, at the request of Acme Soap, has determined the best phrase to use on product packaging. The agency recommends that "The Finnish Fresh Soap" be used. To support this recommendation, the agency cites the results of extensive research which indicate "The Finnish Fresh Soap" is the best descriptive phrase. The research included a positioning study, consideration of alternatives, evaluation of industry standards, consultation with expert opinion, and a check of FTC/FCC guidelines.

The agency believes that the phrase, "The Finnish Fresh Soap," is a strong enough asset to Acme to warrant management's support for keeping it as the package copy.

The agency feels that this will launch the product in the strongest fashion.

INTRODUCTION

ABC Agency was requested by Acme Soap to determine the most effective phrase to use as the descriptive statement on the soap package. To this end, the agency conducted a positioning study, considered alternatives, researched industry standards, consulted expert opinion and checked the FTC/FCC guidelines concerning its recommendation. The agency is confident that all issues have been considered.

Acme Soap was positioned as a refreshment/Finnish Fresh soap in several advertising concepts tested in 1984. The winning concept referred to Acme Soap as "Finnish Fresh," and that description was adopted in subsequent creative and package design development.

During the corporate copy approval process for testing commercial production, the Acme lawyers would permit "Acme, the Finnish Fresh Soap" in the commercial copy but had reservations about allowing it to appear on the package. At that point, the agency complied with your request to submit package copy alternatives, should the "Finnish Fresh" description be disallowed. Although the agency submitted the requested alternatives, it maintained that "Finnish Fresh" was superior to any of the alternatives and should be retained if at all possible.

The legal issue about the package copy has now been cleared. The Acme test commercials are ready for copy testing and the marketing plan is ready for presentation to top management.

FINDINGS

The phrase "The Finnish Fresh Soap" should be maintained on the package for the following reasons:

1) The positioning study reveals a positive sales impact.
2) Alternatives are not as effective as the existing phrase.
3) This phrase uniquely positions Acme Soap.
4) Experts like this phrase.
5) Continuity should be maintained.
6) This phrase does not violate FTC/FCC guidelines.

DETAILED FINDINGS

1. <u>The positioning study test results dramatically demonstrate the positive sales impact of "The Finnish Fresh Soap" phrase</u>. Describing Acme as "The Finnish Fresh Soap" proved to make a significant difference in purchase intent in the 1984 Acme Soap Positioning Study. The approach was exactly the same in all the tests except that the headline was changed for each alternate concept. "The Finnish Fresh Soap" drew a positive purchase intent of 68%, highest of

all, while "The Soap as Refreshing as Finland" was lowest at 55%. (See Exhibit 1, Appendix.)

2. <u>The proposed alternates to "The Finnish Fresh Soap" were less attractive than "The Finnish Fresh Soap</u>." The client-preferred one, "Refreshment like Finland," is similar to the lowest ranking concept on purchase intent and was eliminated.

3. <u>"The Finnish Fresh Soap" description uniquely positions Acme Soap and epitomizes that positioning</u>. Although competition is strong in this field, "The Finnish Fresh Soap" phrase drew positive attention in our study. We believe the shortest, most direct and best method of describing Acme's products and style is "The Finnish Fresh Soap."

4. <u>Experts as well as consumers like the phrase "The Finnish Fresh Soap" and feel that the phrase should be used on packages as well as</u> <u>in advertising</u>. Our advertising and public relations people are the best in the business, and they call the phrase direct, clear and memorable and state that it creates pleasing mental associations. English Professor Emeritus Benjamin Nick of Colgate University, author of <u>Word Connotations</u>, agrees that the emotional associations attached to these words are "fresh, friendly, clean and attractive." The psychology of association is powerful, and once the consumer has associated "The Finnish Fresh Soap" phrase with the product through the advertising, he/she will want to see it on the package.

5. <u>Continuity should be maintained between the package and the</u> <u>commercial message and between past experience and future expansion</u>. The Acme copy capitalizes on the proven strength of "The Finnish Fresh Soap." Over seven million dollars will be spent during the introductory year to deliver this message to consumers. When consumers get to the grocery shelf, they should see the crystallization of the Acme message, "The Finnish Fresh Soap," on the package.

6. <u>The agency's lawyers hold that the "Finnish Fresh Soap" phrase does not violate any FTC/FCC guidelines or standards</u>.  (See Exhibit 2, Appendix.)

RECOMMENDATION

The agency recommends that the current Acme package copy, "Acme, The Finnish Fresh Soap" be maintained as the sole descriptive statement on the package.  We recommend presentation of the concept to management.

APPENDIX

The Appendix is not included in this sample report.

Chapter 9

# Special Management Reports

Now that you have learned the techniques for producing a formal report—adaptable to any topic—it is time to look at a few special reports which you may be called upon to write. These include departmental and research status reports, progress reports, research report summaries, and management recommendations. Of these, the last is probably the most important document that you will be called upon to write. It gives management the benefit of your judgment, and therefore carries a lot of weight. First, however, let's look at the other reports.

## DEPARTMENTAL AND RESEARCH STATUS REPORTS

These are issued periodically, usually in memo form. The readers of these memos may include top management as well as middle-level executives. They are designed to keep these managers informed of the progress and activities in various departments. The basic features of each are summarized below.

### Departmental Status Reports

Status reports keep top management abreast of significant developments in your department—progress, problems, opportunities.

Write it just as you would a memo, but with enough clear headings to guide the executive to particular areas of interest. When possible, keep headings consistent from one report to the next—it saves time for both you and your readers. Below is a sample of a departmental status report.

```
                              MEMO
Date: 1/31/85
To: John Doe
From: Jane Smith, Order Department


Subject:  Departmental Status Report


New Orders: The increase in new orders for the month of
December is 3%.


New Staff: The two new staff members are working out well.


Computer System: The Order Department has fully implemented
the computer system.  All incoming orders are now being
processed through the computer terminals by the new staff.
The orders at this time are approximately ten days behind
due to start up time and training time needed to implement
this new system.  I estimate that within six weeks we will
have eliminated the backlog and will be processing orders
the same day they come in.  The budget allocation for the
computer implementation has been depleted, and there are
approximately $1,000 worth of supplies still needed which
we can purchase out of our supplies budget.
```

## Progress Reports

When you are involved in a major project, management may want to know how it is coming along. This calls for a progress report. Like any other document, the progress report should be clear, direct, specific, and well organized. It should be presented in memo or letter form (depending on whether it is going to people inside or outside the firm), and it should be as brief as possible. When you go about organizing this report, keep in mind that your reader is concerned with what has been accomplished so far, what you are working on currently, what needs to be done, and when it must be completed.

Start the progress report with a statement explaining the problem and the reason it is being studied. This assures the reader that you understand the task. Then go on to tell how you intend to get the information required (method and procedures) and why you are using that approach. Be specific in your information; it is imperative that you understand each other now in order to avoid discovering you each had different interpretations of the task after the report is issued.

If you are far enough along to have formulated some tentative conclusions, share them with the reader. Again, your purpose should be to make sure you are both following the same approach. The progress report is the place to discuss any problems you are encountering. They should be put forward in a positive tone, and accompanied by a list of the solutions you have attempted or planned.

The importance of maintaining a positive tone applies to the report as a whole—whether or not you have run into problems. Your aim should be to convince the reader that you are moving along the right track and making solid progress. Reinforce his confidence that the right person has been selected for the task. End the report with a confirmation of the due date for the final report. A sample progress report is presented below.

```
                              MEMO
DATE: December 12, 1985
TO: Jane Doe
FROM: John Smith
SUBJECT: Progress Report on Client Preference Survey


The test was conducted from November 10 through December
12.  Eighty percent of all clients were contacted. The
responses have been recorded. Tabulation will begin Monday.
This is expected to require approximately five working
days. Analysis will then take place the following week.
This should give us plenty of time to get the
recommendation to you by January 2.
```

## Research Report Summaries

You may be asked to summarize and interpret reports that were conducted for your department's benefit.

To prepare for such an assignment, review Chapter 8 (on how to write a formal report). Pay particular attention to the guidelines on writing conclusions and recommendations, since this is what you will actually be doing. Remember that you are trying not only to impart information but to persuade as well. Therefore, ask yourself the following questions as you write:

- Do the facts justify the conclusions?
- Is each conclusion supported by a brief statement reinforcing its validity?
- Are the recommendations appropriate to the problems or situations being studied?
- Is the entire report written in a logical, persuasive manner? Is it easy to follow, with no surprises to break the flow?

A sample report summary appears below.

## Research Report Summary

Summary of Acme Soap Positioning Study

The report of the ABC Agency strongly recommends that the phrase "The Finnish Fresh Soap" should be maintained as the sole descriptive statement on the package.

The positioning study test results dramatically demonstrate the positive sales impact of "The Finnish Fresh Soap" phrase. Describing Acme as "The Finnish Fresh Soap" proved to make a significant difference in purchase intent in the 1984 Acme Soap Positioning Study. Specifically, the winning concept, using a refreshment positioning with "The Finnish Fresh Soap" headline, had a positive purchase intent of 68%. In contrast, the concept with the lowest purchase interest of all the approaches was exactly the same as the winning concept, except that the headline was replaced with "The Soap as Refreshing as Finland." This version had a positive purchase intent of only 55%.

Of the several alternate phrases offered, the client-preferred one is "Refreshment like Finland." Reviewing the Positioning Study concepts, however, we find that "The Soap as Refreshing As Finland" was the concept ranking lowest on purchase intent.

"The Finnish Fresh Soap" seems the best choice. It uniquely positions Acme Soap and epitomizes that positioning. Our attorneys' objections have been settled. "The Finnish Fresh Soap" is our most likely route to a successful product launch.

## MANAGEMENT RECOMMENDATIONS

This may be the most important writing you do, because a management recommendation is the document used to convey your thoughts and proposals to your superiors. In some cases, your success or failure may hinge on the way you handle this task, and—as with any important assignment—you should take your time and study the matter before you begin. Don't be concerned if it takes a long time to write a good recommendation: even experienced managers find that they end up writing several drafts before their recommendation is ready for submission to top management.

## Format

A "management recommendation" should be divided into four parts: background, recommendation, rationale, and discussion. It is similar to a Type II formal report (see Chapter 8) in that the recommended action is stated before the supporting facts.

**Background.** This section corresponds to the "Introduction" and "Background" sections of a full-scale report, discussed earlier. (See Chapter 8.) It should give the reader everything needed to understand the recommendation. Include a statement of the problem, why the recommendation is being offered, and any background information which will lead to the recommendation.

**Recommendation.** Just as with a formal report, this is the heart of the document. In it you give your opinion of what to do about the situation. It should be:

- Positively stated,
- Within the range of possibility,
- Supported by a factual analysis (or at least a logical one), and
- Well supported by the rationale.

**Rationale.** This corresponds to a combination of the "Conclusions" and "Summary of Findings" in a formal report, because each point in the rationale is a conclusion (judgment) supported by a finding (fact). The rationale presents an argument, in several numbered steps, which leads up to the recommendation. Therefore, your strongest, most compelling points in the rationale should be presented first. Consider it as taking your reader through the thought process which led you to your recommendation. Turn to the annotated example of a well developed rationale at the end of this chapter. Notice that the conclusion is underscored, followed by the findings which support it.

**Discussion.** This usually takes the argument one step further by assuring the reader of the writer's commitment to the recommendation. It urges support for the measure being recommended and may ask for management's aid in pushing the project forward.

## General Guidelines

A management recommendation should reflect your most logical thinking, starting with an analysis of the problem and ending with suggested solutions and the reasoning behind them. If you can keep distracting thoughts to a minimum and avoid going off on tangents, you'll be able to put forth a cogent argument that is sure to impress management favorably.

When submitting recommendations based on a research report (that is, when you have reviewed the research and decided what action should be taken) think of the recommendation as skimming the cream off the study. Take only the "richest" or most significant information and add to it a summary of your own thinking on the matter. The fact that your recommendations will be read by management warrants putting forth a special effort. There will be times when management recommendations do not spring from a particular body of research but grow out of situations in the company calling for improvement or corrective action. When you are writing a recommendation under these circumstances, be careful in selecting data and opinions to support your thinking. It's all too easy to turn the recommendations into a vehicle for expressing your own ideas or instincts in the matter—which are seldom enough to elicit management's support. Cite past experience, existing studies, expert opinion, projections based on experience or logic, and any other objective sources you can find to build a convincing case.

The management recommendation is an extremely useful, effective and flexible document. It is your channel to the top of the company—use it well and wisely.

Following is the management recommendation urging adoption of the phrase. "The Finnish Fresh Soap," to be used in package copy for Acme Soap (see sample report, Chapter 8), submitted to top management by the product manager.

ACME Letterhead

## Proposal on Acme Soap Package Copy

Based on my assessment of the ABC Advertising Agency's study and resulting recommendation, I request that you consider the phrase "The Finnish Fresh Soap" to be used on Acme Soap package copy.

BACKGROUND

We contracted the ABC Advertising Agency on December 20, 1984 to conduct a study to determine the most effective phrase to use on Acme Soap's package. Several advertising concepts tested in 1984 referred to Acme Soap as "Finnish Fresh." The phrase was adopted in subsequent package design development, but the company attorneys would not permit "Acme, the Finnish Fresh Soap" on the package.

RECOMMENDATION

On the basis of the report submitted by the agency, I recommend that "Acme, The Finnish Fresh Soap" be approved as the sole descriptive statement on the package.

RATIONALE

The positioning study test results show that "The Finnish Fresh Soap" has the best positive sales impact. According to the report, this phrase showed a positive purchase intent of 68%, whereas alternates tested lower.

The proposed alternates are similar to the descriptions used in the positioning study. They were judged as not as strong as the recommended phrase. Of the several alternates offered, we preferred "Refreshment like Finland." However, after reviewing the Positioning Study concepts, we find that "The Soap as Refreshing As Finland" was the concept ranking lowest on purchase intent. "The Finnish Fresh Soap," therefore, can be assumed to be stronger.

In accordance with company standards, continuity should be maintained between the package and commercial message. "The Finnish Fresh Soap" has proven to be a strong commercial message.

In my judgment as well as the judgment of the agency, the shortest, most direct and impactful method of stating Acme's proposition is "The Finnish Fresh Soap."

The report states that agency has determined that the "Finnish Fresh Soap" phrase does not violate any FTC/FCC guidelines or standards. Further, given their experience and knowledge of the FTC, they do not feel that this is likely to be the type of thing that the FTC would choose as a target.

DISCUSSION

The agency believes that "The Finnish Fresh Soap" is a strong enough asset to Acme to warrant your support for keeping it as the package copy. This will probably mean a product management commitment to use the phrase on the package.

Please consider this recommendation, and let me know your decision. We're all anxious to move the project ahead. I am convinced that if you approve of this recommendation the project will be launched in the strongest fashion.

Sincerely,

(signed by the product manager)

# Section IV

# Writers' Appendices

# Appendix I

# Trite Word/Phrase Replacements

Increase the impact of your business writing by replacing trite words and phrases with fresher, more to-the-point phrasing. Use this chart to help you get started.

| TRITE WORD/PHRASE | REPLACEMENT |
|---|---|
| above mentioned/aforementioned | this/these |
| according to our records | we find |
| acknowledge receipt of | we received |
| advise | say/tell |
| after very careful consideration | after considering |
| ahead of schedule | early |
| along the lines of | like |
| at all times | always |
| at such time | when |
| at the present/at this time | now |
| at your earliest convenience | soon/immediately (or specify date) |
| attached you will find | attached is |
| be in a position to | able to/can |
| despite the fact that | although/even though |
| due to the fact that | because |
| enclosed you will find | here is/enclosed is |
| for the purpose of | for |
| hereto/herewith | omit—it is usually unnecessary |
| in accordance with | as/by |

| TRITE WORD/PHRASE | REPLACEMENT |
|---|---|
| in order that | so |
| in re | regarding/concerning |
| in the amount of | for |
| in the event that | if/in case |
| in the near future | soon |
| in view of | because |
| is of the opinion | thinks/feels/believes |
| of a confidential nature | confidential |
| our files/records indicate | we find |
| owing to the fact that | because |
| subsequent to | after |
| take into consideration | consider |
| we are in receipt of | we have |

## Appendix II

# Punctuation Rules

Punctuation is an aid to clarity. It can re-create some of the characteristics of speech—pitch, intonation, pause and stress—and help bring the impact of the spoken word to the printed page.

Punctuation should not be used to patch up an awkward sentence. It is always better to rephrase rather than to overpunctuate. Aim for simplicity and clarity, and use punctuation judiciously. The trend is to use fewer breaks in the writing flow (particularly commas) to facilitate reading and aid clarity.

This appendix lists various punctuation marks and the usage for each. Examples appear after each rule.

## Apostrophe

An apostrophe is used to convey the idea of ownership or possession—hence the term, "possessive noun."

Add "'s" when the noun is singular and does not end in "s." When it does end in "s" (or in an "s" sound), you may add simply an apostrophe or an apostrophe and "s."

- child's
- man's
- boss'
- boss's

Plural nouns ending in "s" take an apostrophe to make them possessive, while those not ending in "s" take an apostrophe and "s."

- waiters'

- men's

When compound nouns are involved, add the "s" to the word nearest to the thing possessed.

- The inspector general's report

Show joint possession by adding "'s" to the last word of a pair or series. To show individual possession, an apostrophe is placed after each item.

- Men and women's salaries were raised; ("salaries" refers to both equally.)
- Men's and women's salaries are frequently unequal (shows a separation between the two salaries.)

Sometimes a possessive form is used even though there is no actual ownership.

- three weeks' time

Where the form suggests possession but is really descriptive, omit the apostrophe.

- editors handbook

Apostrophes are used to indicate contractions, omission of letters or figures, and often form plurals of letters, figures and abbreviations.

- it's, can't, ma'am
- p's and q's
- summer of '56
- 2200 r.p.m.'s

## Brackets

Use brackets to indicate parentheses within parentheses: ([ ])

Brackets are used to indicate additions to quoted material, either for clarity, explanation or editorial comment.

- He wrote, "I recieved [sic] your letter."

## Colon

Colons are used to suggest that something is to follow, be it an explanation, list, or example.

- The evidence was everywhere: on the walls, on the floor and in the sink.

In business letters, a colon follows the salutation, and also goes between the initials of the writer and typist at the end of the letter.

## Comma

A comma is used to separate sections of a sentence. The trend is to omit optional commas to improve readability. Unless they are needed for clarity, leave them out.

## Appendix II–Punctuation Rules

Use a comma to separate items in a series. When a conjunction joins the last two elements in a series, the comma may be omitted.

- He set the objectives, strategy, tactics(,) and budget for the campaign.

A comma separates adjectives and phrases of equal weight modifying the same word. However, two or more tightly connected adjectives in series, each modifying the same word or phrase, may not require punctuation.

- The large, brown, heavy parcel looked mysterious.
- The issue rested on whether the 90-cubic yard waterproof tank was large enough.

Use a comma before the conjunction in a compound sentence, unless the sentence is very brief.

- He would have made the meeting, but he had to go out of town.
- He arrived late and he left early.

A comma can indicate omission of a verb in the second part of a compound sentence.

- He chose the short form; his friend, the long.

Insert a comma after an introductory clause or phrase unless it is short enough to leave no chance of misunderstanding.

- Unless inflation abates in the next year, money will be tighter.
- After cutting the budget they increased profits.

Place commas before and after nonrestrictive clauses. Nonrestrictive clauses, though informative, are not absolutely necessary to the understanding of the sentence.

- Harold Pinter, the famous playwright, wrote "The Homecoming."

Very short clauses forming a series and not joined by a conjunction may be separated by commas.

- He arrived, he looked around, he left quickly.

Set off "yes" or "no" when used as interjections (introductory words). The same goes for other mild interjections, such as "well."

- Yes, you may go.

Unless it is very short, an adverbial clause that precedes a main clause is set off by a comma. (An adverbial clause functions like an adverb, but contains a subject and verb of its own).

- If you expect to succeed, you must work very hard.

Parenthetical expressions (words or phrases that interrupt the flow of a sentence and that can be omitted without altering the meaning of the sentence) are set off by commas. Examples include appositives (words or phrases that identify or supplement the preceding noun), people addressed, items in addresses and dates and independent phrases and clauses.

- Ms. Johnson, the new supervisor, had decided to quit.
- Sam, what time is it?
- She left for Boston, Massachusetts, yesterday.
- She was, everyone thought, a very dependable person.

A direct quotation is usually separated from the rest of the sentence by a comma. An exception to this is when the quotation is so closely connected to the rest of the sentence that no comma is required. Remember that commas are always placed inside closing quotes.

- "Stop right here," he demanded.
- His warning was always "watch the bottom line!"

Items in a date are separated by commas, but when only the month and year are used, the comma between them is optional.

- May 16, 1946, was her birthday.
- May 1946 was very warm.

Commas are used after the complimentary close in business letters, between a name and a title that follows it, and between a title and the name of the organization when "of" or "of the" is omitted.

- Donald Denton, Ph.D.
- Deputy, Fire Department

Use a comma to separate thousands, millions, etc. in numerals, but when only four digits are involved, the comma is optional.

- 166,000,908 but $2342

## Dash

A dash is formed by two consecutive hyphens (--) when using a standard typewriter. When documents are typeset, a dash appears as a solid line (—). Dashes are used to indicate a sudden break or shift in thought, an appositive, or special emphasis.

- "Now if we can just—what was that noise?"
- The frontier—everything west of the Mississippi—presented even greater hazards.

## Ellipsis Points

Use three spaced periods (. . .), called ellipsis points to indicate omissions from a quotation. When the ellipsis points end a sentence, add one more period.

- "Should rates continue to climb . . . we can increase profits."
- "Next year, things will be different . . . . "

## Exclamation Point

An exclamation point, followed by two spaces, is used to end a sentence that expresses strong feeling. The sentence can be in the form of a command, question, or statement.

- Fire!
- How could he do something like that!
- He just can't fail!

Exclamation points should be used sparingly. Overuse dilutes their impact.

## Hyphen

Hyphens are used to divide a word when it will not fit on one line. Use a hyphen when a number or letter modifies a spelled-out word.

- 6-room apartment, T-square, U-turn

Unless they are absolutely necessary for clarity, hyphens can be eliminated between a prefix and a root word, unless the root is a proper noun or adjective. Usage can vary here, so it's best to consult a dictionary.

- antiwar, nonviolent
- un-American

Hyphenate a phrase used as a single modifier.

- Everyone knows the famous ta-ta-ta-tum passage in Beethoven's Fifth.
- It was the one-big-happy-family atmosphere that made all the difference.

## Italics/Underscore

Titles of books, magazines, newspapers, plays and motion pictures should be underscored or set in italics. Names of ships, aircraft, spacecraft and titles of works of art are also underscored.

Legal cases are usually italicized.

Underscoring is also used to indicate words that should be stressed and foreign words not in common usage in our language:

- "_Stop!_" he screamed.
- It was a _bete noir_.

## Parentheses

Information that is helpful, but not mandatory to understanding the sentence, is enclosed in parentheses.

When numbered items are listed in a sentence, use parentheses to isolate the numbers.

- He wanted everyone to (1) be on time, (2) take notes and (3) think!

Explanatory words not included in the quotation are enclosed in parentheses.

- She explained, "We found him in a restaurant just over the Springfield (Mass.) line."

## Period

Use a period, with two spaces after it, to end:

- A declarative sentence. Example: (Inflation is a worldwide problem.)
- An imperative sentence. Example: (Order new stationery.)

Use a period after initials and abbreviations, followed by one space.

- H. G. Wellman
- California Ave.

Use a period without a space after it as a decimal point.

- 3.5 mills, $18.75

Use a period after Roman numerals and letters in an outline, but not in titles or in the middle of text.

- I. Objectives
- Queen Elizabeth II
- The answer can be found in Volume II, but only if you know where to look.

## Question Mark

Use a question mark, followed by two spaces, after a direct question or at the end of a sentence that asks a question, even if in a declarative form.

- How can you say that?
- The rates are too high?

When a sentence contains both factual and interrogative elements, choose the punctuation that agrees with the last clause.

- She has always performed very well, so why not promote her?

Use a question mark to indicate doubt about the accuracy of a statement.

- There are 345 (?) items in the list.

## Quotation Marks

Enclose direct quotations and fragments of exactly quoted matter in quotation marks.

- He asked, "What is the budget?"
- The contract stated "the agreement will be executed in ten days" after the first meeting.

Enclose unfamiliar or unusual phrases or words, technical terms, words or phrases that define or explain, and special usages in quotation marks—but guard against overuse of this style.

Enclose titles of catalogues, reports, articles, book chapters, songs, lectures, and short musical pieces in quotation marks.

Use single quotes to indicate a quotation inside a quotation.

- She said, "He specifically stated, 'This is high enough,' for the 1985 sales forecast."

Short quotes are enclosed in quotation marks and run in the normal text.

For long quotes, indent both margins and single space, omitting quotation marks.

Punctuation accompanying quotation marks varies:

Put periods and commas inside closing quotes, and colons and semicolons outside them.

Place dashes, question marks, exclamation points and closing parentheses inside closing quotes when they only pertain to the quoted material. When they pertain to the entire sentence, then go outside the closing quotes.

## Semicolon

Think of a semicolon as a weak period or a strong comma. When a period is acceptable or appropriate, do not substitute a semicolon. When a comma does not adequately separate thoughts, use a semicolon.

When two sentences are closely related, use a semicolon rather than a period.

- He made money in the stock market; he lost it on real estate.

When adverbs such as "also," "therefore," "hence," and "meanwhile" are used to join two thoughts, a semicolon frequently precedes the adverb.

- She had a firm grasp of economics; therefore, she performed very well in the examination. (For added emphasis on the connective adverb, a comma is usually placed after it.)

Use a semicolon to separate compound sentences when either or both clauses contain commas. A semicolon is also used to separate items in a series that already contains commas.

- There were several things of note in the lecture: first, the financial setup, including the cash flow position; second, the economic outlook for the 90-day, 6-month and one year terms; and last, the computerized systems to administer the plan.

A semicolon is frequently used before "for example," "e.g.," "that is," "namely," and "viz.," when they introduce a series.

# Appendix III

# Formal Forms of Address

| ADDRESSEE | ENVELOPE & INSIDE ADDRESS | SALUTATION | COMPLIMENTARY CLOSE |
|---|---|---|---|
| **EDUCATION:** | | | |
| Chancellor (of a university) | Dr. John/Jane Doe<br>Chancellor<br>Name of university | Dear Sir/Madam: | Very truly yours, |
| Chaplain (of a college or university) | The Reverend John/Jane Doe<br>Chaplain<br>Name of college/university | Dear Chaplain Doe: | Respectfully yours, |
| Dean (Of a college or university) | Dean John/Jane Doe<br>Name of college/university<br>or<br>Dr. John/Jane Doe, Dean | Dear Sir/Madam:<br>or<br>Dear Dean Doe | Very truly yours, |
| Instructor | Dr./Mr./Ms. John/Jane Doe<br>Instructor<br>Name of college/university | Dear Sir/Madam:<br>or<br>Dear Dr./Mr./Ms. Doe | Very truly yours, |
| President (of a college or university | Dr./Mr./Ms. John/Jane Doe<br>President<br>Name of college/university | Dear Sir/Madam: | Very truly yours, |
| (if priest) | The Very Reverend John Doe, S.J.<br><br>President<br>Name of college/university | Dear Sir: | Very truly yours, |

| ADDRESSEE | ENVELOPE & INSIDE ADDRESS | SALUTATION | COMPLIMENTARY CLOSE |
|---|---|---|---|
| Professor (full): | Professor John/Jane Doe<br>or<br>Professor of _____<br>Name of university | Dear Sir/Madam:<br>Dear Professor Doe:<br>Dear Dr. Doe | Very truly yours, |
| Professor (assistant or associate) | Dr./Mr./Ms. John/Jane Doe<br>Assistant/Associate Professor of____<br>name of university | Dear Dr./Mr./Ms./ Doe:<br>or<br>Dear Professor Doe: | Very truly yours,<br><br>Sincerely yours, |

**GOVERNMENT: Consulate/Diplomatic**

| | | | |
|---|---|---|---|
| American Consulate | The American Consulate<br>foreign city, country<br><br>(In Central/South America):<br>The Consulate of the United States of America<br>city, country<br>America | Gentlemen: | Very truly yours, |
| Foreign Consulate | The (country) Consulate<br>city, state | Gentlemen: | Very truly yours, |
| American Ambassador | The Honorable John/Jane Doe<br>American Ambassador<br>(In Central/South America):<br>The Ambassador of the United States of America<br>city, country | Sir/Madam: | Very truly yours, |
| Foreign Ambassador | His/Her Excellency John/Jane Doe, Ambassador of (country)<br>(If from Gt. Britain):<br>His/Her Excellency<br>The Right Honorable John/Jane Doe, British Ambassador | Excellency:<br><br>Excellency: | Very truly yours,<br><br>Very truly yours, |
| American Minister | The Honorable John/Jane Doe<br>American Minister<br>(If in Central/South America):<br>Minister of the United States of America<br>city, country | Sir/Madam: | Very truly yours |
| Foreign Minister | The Honorable John/Jane Doe<br>Minister of _____<br>city, country | Sir/Madam: | Very truly yours, |

**GOVERNMENT: Foreign Heads of State**

| | | | |
|---|---|---|---|
| Premier | His/Her Excellency John/Jane Doe<br>Premier of (country)<br>city, country | Excellency: | Respectfully yours, |

*Appendix III–Formal Forms of Address*

| ADDRESSEE | ENVELOPE & INSIDE ADDRESS | SALUTATION | COMPLIMENTARY CLOSE |
|---|---|---|---|
| President of a Republic | His/Her Excellency John/Jane Doe President of (country) city, country | Excellency: | Respectfully yours, |
| Prime Minister | His/Her Excellency John/Jane Doe Prime Minister of (country city, country | Excellency: | Respectfully yours, |

**GOVERNMENT: U. S. Federal**

| ADDRESSEE | ENVELOPE & INSIDE ADDRESS | SALUTATION | COMPLIMENTARY CLOSE |
|---|---|---|---|
| Attorney General | The Honorable John/Jane Doe The Attorney General city, state | Sir/Madam: | Very truly yours, |
| Cabinet Officer addressed as Secretary | The Honorable John/Jane Doe Secretary of (department) city, state | Sir/Madam: | Very truly yours, |
| Chairman of a (sub) committee, U.S. Congress | The Honorable John/Jane Doe Chairman, Committee on (name) United States Senate/House of Representatives Washington, DC | Dear Mr./Madam Chairman: | Very truly yours, |
| Commissioner | (If appointed): The Honorable John/Jane Doe Commissioner city, state | Dear Mr./Madam Commissioner: | Very truly yours, |
| | If career): Mr./Ms. John/Jane DoeDear Mr./Ms. Doe Commissioner | Very truly yours, | |
| Congressman/woman: U.S. Congress Representative | The Honorable John/Jane Doe United States House of Representatives | Dear Sir/Madam: | Very truly yours, |
| U.S. Senator | The Honorable John/Jane Doe United States Senate | Sir/Madam: | Very truly yours, |
| Director (of an independent agency): | The Honorable John/Jane Doe Director (name) Agency | Dear Mr./Ms. Doe: | Very truly yours, |
| Postmaster General | The Honorable John/Jane Doe The Postmaster General | Sir/Madam: | Very truly yours, |
| President-elect of the U.S. | The Honorable John/Jane Doe President-elect of the United States city, state | Dear Sir/Madam: | Very truly yours, |
| President | The President The White House Washington, DC. | Mr./Ms. President: | Respectfully yours, |

| ADDRESSEE | ENVELOPE & INSIDE ADDRESS | SALUTATION | COMPLIMENTARY CLOSE |
|---|---|---|---|
| President (former) | The Honorable John/Jane Doe<br>city, state | Sir/Madam: | Respectfully yours, |
| Press Secretary to the President | Mr./Ms. John/Jane Doe<br>Press Secretary to the President | Dear Mr./Ms. Doe: | Very truly yours, |
| Vice President | The Vice President of the United States<br>United States Senate<br>Washington, DC | Sir/Madam: | Respectfully, |

### GOVERNMENT: U. S. Local

| ADDRESSEE | ENVELOPE & INSIDE ADDRESS | SALUTATION | COMPLIMENTARY CLOSE |
|---|---|---|---|
| Alderman | The Honorable John/Jane Doe<br>Alderman<br>city, state | Dear Mr./Ms. Doe | Very truly yours, |
| City Attorney (city counsel, corporation counsel) | The Honorable John/Jane Doe<br>City Attorney<br>city, state | Dear Mr./Ms. Doe | Very truly yours |
| County Clerk | The Honorable John/Jane Doe<br>Clerk of (name) County<br>city, state | Dear Mr./Ms. Doe: | Very truly yours, |
| Judge | The Honorable John/Jane Doe<br>Judge of the (name)<br>Court of (name)<br>city, state | Dear Judge Doe: | Very truly yours, |
| Mayor | The Honorable John/Jane Doe<br>Mayor of (city)<br>city, state | Sir/Madam: | Very truly yours, |

### GOVERNMENT: State Officials

| ADDRESSEE | ENVELOPE & INSIDE ADDRESS | SALUTATION | COMPLIMENTARY CLOSE |
|---|---|---|---|
| Attorney | The Honorable John/Jane Doe<br>(title)<br>city, state | Dear Mr./Ms. Doe: | Very truly yours, |
| Attorney General | The Honorable John/Jane Doe<br>Attorney General of the State of (state name)<br>city, state | Sir/Madam: | Very truly yours, |
| Clerk of a Court | John/Jane Doe, Esq.<br>Clerk of the Court of (name)<br>city, state | Dear Mr./Ms. Doe | Very truly yours, |
| Governor | The Honorable John/Jane Doe<br>Governor of (state)<br>city, state | Sir/Madam: | Respectfully yours, |

*Appendix III–Formal Forms of Address*

| ADDRESSEE | ENVELOPE & INSIDE ADDRESS | SALUTATION | COMPLIMENTARY CLOSE |
|---|---|---|---|
| Lieutenant Governor | The honorable John/Jane Doe<br>Lieutenant Governor of (state)<br>city, state | Sir/Madam: | Respectfully yours, |
| Representative (including assemblyman, delegate) | The Honorable John/Jane Doe<br>House of Representatives<br>(of The State Assembly/House of Delegates)<br>city, state | Sir/Madam: | Very truly yours, |
| Secretary of State | The Honorable John/Jane Doe<br>Secretary of State of (state)<br>city, state | Sir/Madam: | Very truly yours, |
| Senator | The Honorable John/Jane Doe<br>The Senate of (state)<br>city, state | Sir/Madam: | Very truly yours, |
| Speaker (state assembly, house of delegates or house of representatives) | The Honorable John/Jane Doe<br>Speaker of (body)<br>city, state | Sir/Madam: | Very truly yours, |

## LEGAL OFFICIALS

| ADDRESSEE | ENVELOPE & INSIDE ADDRESS | SALUTATION | COMPLIMENTARY CLOSE |
|---|---|---|---|
| Federal Judge | The Honorable John/Jane Doe<br>Judge of the United States District Court for the (name) District of (name)<br>city, state | Sir/Madam: | Very truly yours, |
| Supreme Court, Associate Justice | Mr./Ms. Justice Doe<br>The Supreme Court of the United States<br>Washington, DC | Sir/Madam: | Very truly yours, |
| Supreme Court, Chief Justice | The Chief Justice of the United States<br>The Supreme Court of the United States<br>Washington, DC | Sir/Madam: | Respectfully, |
| Judge, state court | The Honorable John/Jane Doe<br>Judge of the (title) Court<br>city, state | Dear Judge Doe: | Very truly yours, |
| Supreme Court, State, Chief/Associate Justice | The Honorable John/Jane Doe<br>Chief/Associate Justice of the Supreme Court of (state)<br>city, state | Sir/Madam: | Very truly yours, |

# Appendix IV

# Footnotes and Bibliographies

## FOOTNOTES

Footnotes are used to indicate that certain material has either been directly quoted or paraphrased. The purpose is twofold: to give the quoted person or source credit for the thought and to tell the reader where he can obtain further information.

When a footnote is required, it is marked by an Arabic numeral slightly above the writing line directly after the quoted material. Numbers run consecutively from the start to the end of the report. (If preferred, numbers can begin anew in each chapter.) Footnotes can be placed at the bottom of the page on which they appear (separated from the text by a 2" line at the left margin), or in a group at the end of the report. Whichever style you use, make sure that it is consistent throughout the document. A footnote at the bottom of the page begins with the applicable superscript Arabic numeral, indented slightly from the left margin, while succeeding lines of the footnote start on the left margin. The superscript is not separated from the author's name. Single space each footnote, but double space between notes. A full footnote contains all of the information listed below that applies to the work being cited.

## Book

- Author's full name(s)—if more than three, follow first author's name with et al.
- Complete title of the book, underscored
- Editor, compiler or translator
- Name of the series containing the book, and volume number
- Edition, if not the first
- Location and name of publisher
- Date of publication
- Page number(s) from which the quoted material was taken.

**Example:**
[1]Robert L. Shurter, J. Peter Williamson and Wayne G. Broehl, Business Reseach and Report Writing (New York: McGraw-Hill Book Company, 1965), p. 16.

Notice that parentheses surround the publishing identification, while commas separate the other elements. All bibliographical entries close with a period.

## Periodical

- Author's full name(s)
- Title of article, in quotation marks
- Name of periodical, underscored
- Volume and number of the periodical
- Month, day and year of issue
- Page number(s)

**Magazine:**
[1]Astin Jones, "New Horizons," Modern Science, Dec., 1977, pp. 12-25.

**Newspaper:**
[1]Avril Smith, "Progress in Washington," Washington Post, Aug. 30, 1977, p. 46, cols. 3-4.

## Unpublished Material

- Author's name, if known
- Title of document, in quotation marks

- Nature of the material (letter, dissertation, etc.)
- Folio or other identification number
- Name of collection from which the material was taken
- Geographical location of collection
- Date of issue

**Manuscript:**
[1]Gen. Stanley Freh, "Report to the War Committee, 18 Feb. 1926," Military Records Division, Record Group 56, National Archives, Washington, DC.

**Letter:**
[1]John Doe, personal letter.

**Speech:**
[1]Alison Doe, "Dynamics of Econometrics," speech given to Harvard Business Club, New York, Jan. 23, 1980.

**Interview:**
[1]Jane Doe, interview held during meeting of American Management Association, New York, June 6, 1980.

## Subsequent Citations

The above citations refer to the first time the source is cited. Subsequent citations should be stated as follows:

- When the author's name appears in the text, it may be omitted from subsequent references. Just cite book and page:

[2]<u>Business Research and Report Writing,</u> p. 18.

- When the author's name does not appear in the text next to the quote, cite name and page (or name, book and page):

[2]Shurter, Williamson and Broehl, p. 18.

[2]Shurter, Williamson and Broehl, <u>Business Research and Report Writing</u>, p. 18.

- A reference to a formerly quoted article should include the author's last name, title of the article and page number.

[2]Jones, "New Horizons," p. 16.

The preceding formats are gaining widespread acceptance in business reports. There is another method of repeated citation, which is used in formal documents, academic theses and some full-dress reports. It is the Latin abbreviation style, using <u>loc. cit.</u>, <u>op. cit</u> and <u>ibid</u>. The abbreviated citations already given are

*Business Writing Made Simple*

preferable, but you may be called on to use this older, more formal style at some time.

Ibid. (meaning "in the same place") is used when the work being cited is the same as in the immediately preceding footnote:

²Ibid., p. 56.

If the next quote comes from the same source and page, omit the page number:

³Ibid.

Loc. cit. (meaning "in the place cited") and op. cit. (meaning "in the work cited") are used with the author's name, which may appear in the running text or the first time it is cited in a footnote. (In other words, if the author's name is not known or used, you may not use op. cit. or loc. cit.)

²Shurter, Williamson and Broehl, loc. cit., p. 18.

²Shurter, Williamson and Broehl, op. cit.,p. 18.

Remember that loc. cit. may be used only when referring to the same page(s) of the same source cited earlier with other footnotes intervening; op. cit. may be used when referring to different pages of a source cited earlier. Neither abbreviation should be used when you are using material from more than one work by the same author. In that case, use the author, title and page(s) in the citation.

## BIBLIOGRAPHIES

A bibliography is an alphabetical list of the sources used by a writer in preparing a report or other work. An entry should contain all of the following information that applies.

## Books

- Author's name, surname first—if more than three authors, the first is followed by et al.
- Title of the book
- Editor, compiler or translator
- Name of the series in which the book appears
- Volume number
- Edition, if not the first
- Number of volumes, if more than one
- Location and name of publisher
- Date of publication

**Example:**

Shurter, Robert, Williamson, J. Peter, and Broehl, Wayne. <u>Business Research and Report Writing</u>. New York: McGraw-Hill Book Company, 1965.

Notice that periods rather than commas are used to separate author from title and title from publishing information.

## Periodicals

- Author's name, surname first—if more than three authors, the first is followed by <u>et al</u>.
- Title of article, in quotation marks
- Name of periodical, underscored
- Volume and number
- Issue date (month, day, year)
- Page(s)

**Example:**

Jones, Astin. "New Horizons." <u>Modern Science</u>. Dec. 1977, pp. 12-25.

## Unpublished Material

- Author's name, surname first
- Title of document in quotation marks
- Nature of the material (such as letter or dissertation)
- Folio number or other identification number
- Name of collection from which the material was taken
- Geographical location of collection
- Date of issue

**Example: (from a manuscript)**

Freh, Stanley. "Report to the War Committee," Manuscript. Record Group 56, Military Records Division. National Archives: Washington, D. C., Feb. 18, 1926.

Bibliographic entries are not numbered, but are arranged alphabetically by the first item in the reference. The first line of an entry is aligned flush with the left margin, subsequent lines are indented from one to seven spaces, depending on the format of the report—or company policy. Entries are single-spaced, with a double space between entries. Items within an entry are separated by periods. See samples above.

When several works by the same author are used, alphabetize them by title. Entries after the first one by the same author show three hyphens instead of the name, followed by the rest of the entry in standard form.

(Example:--- Book title. Place of Publication: Publisher, Date.)

# Appendix V

# Using Tables and Graphs in Reports

## TABLES

Tables are the easiest and most effective way of presenting a great deal of related data in a concise, accurate, and meaningful way. It is the author's duty to make sure that the tables are clearly interpreted. Don't let the reader guess about what a table is showing—make it clear.

Here are some guidelines to follow in deciding when and how to use tables.

**Size.** Usually, a table is called for when more than three items of information appear which must be related or compared. While tables usually contain numerical data, comparative discussions can often be clarified when advantages and disadvantages are presented in table form.

When a table becomes unwieldy, break it up into sections or its communication value will be lost. Tables that look too complex are likely to be ignored.

**Titles and headings.** Unless a table is very small and appears in the text, it should have a title.

Both columns (across) and rows (down) must have headings. Units of measurement must be clearly identified under each heading. Setting up the table this way eliminates repetitive data (unit of measure) from the table's body, thus consolidating information and adding clarity.

**Footnotes.** To avoid confusion with numerical data in the table, use asterisks to indicate footnotes. This method can be used for up to four footnotes. If more notes are necessary, use letters or consider making another column just for the footnotes.

**Contents.** Resist the temptation to make the report look more "official" or complete by including unnecessary data in the tables. Anything that is not needed to understand the text of the report should be eliminated. Furthermore, anything that is repeated in every column or row should be pulled out of the contents and placed in the heading of that row or column.

When numbers are repeated in a table, one under the other, do not use ditto marks. It can be confusing to the reader. Instead, repeat the entire number. But indicate thousands, millions, etc. with words or grouped zeros ('000) in the headings. When no number appears in a particular spot, indicate this with a dash rather than leaving a blank space. Numbers in columns should be aligned with the decimal point. For a number less than one, place a zero before decimal.

**Layout.** When laying out a table, aim for consistency and an uncluttered appearance. Eliminate clutter by:

- Using clear, concise headings
- Making clear unit notations, accurately placed
- Using correct alignment and grouping of data
- Omitting unnecessary information
- Grouping related data
- Controlling the number of footnotes
- Substituting extra space for grid lines to separate rows and columns
- Separating the title from the body by boldface or underscoring

Column titles go across the top, horizontally, while row titles go down the left-hand margin. The table below demonstrates good layout.

```
              COST PER THOUSAND ANALYSIS
            OF ACME PRODUCTS 1980 MEDIA
```

| Recommended Publications | Circulation (000's) | Effective* Cost per Thousand | |
|---|---|---|---|
| | | Women 18-49 | Married women |
| Atlantic Guide | 1714.5 | $1.35 | $1.69 |
| Home Circle | 8032.1 | 1.36 | 1.36 |
| Modern Shopper | 300.1 | 4.79 | 5.63 |

*Out-of-home readership discounted by 50%

*Appendix V–Using Tables and Graphs in Reports*

## Graphs and Illustrations

A good graph or illustration presents the desired information quickly and clearly. The aim is not so much to be precise as it is to reveal or establish a pattern. In other words, the reader does not need a blueprint complete with specifications; he wants to see the item, not build one from your drawing. The same holds true for graphs: the reader doesn't need to interpolate results to a high degree of accuracy, but he should be able to spot a trend. When mathematical precision is your goal, chart the information or put it in a table.

## Graphs

The trends you are trying to show graphically will be more effectively communicated if the graph is designed according to the following guidelines:

**1. Scale as multiple of 10, and range appropriate to graphed data.** Selection of the scale is probably the single most important factor determining a graph's legibility and clarity. Make it a multiple of 10 whenever possible. The range of the scale (upper and lower limits) should not go beyond the values you are plotting. This means that the starting point is not always zero. Designing the scale so that the curve or lines of the graph fill the entire available space benefits you in three ways: (1) it uses space more efficiently (no large gaps are left); (2) it makes the graph more dramatic, since it occupies the entire area; and (3) it makes the graph look balanced visually.

**2. Axes in standard fashion.** Follow academic tradition when plotting the axes: dependent variable on the ordinate (vertical Y-axis, on the left) and independent variable on the abscissa (horizontal X-axis, on the bottom). Try to lay out the graph as a horizontal rectangle rather than a vertical one, simply to avoid calling attention to the layout at the expense of the data presented.

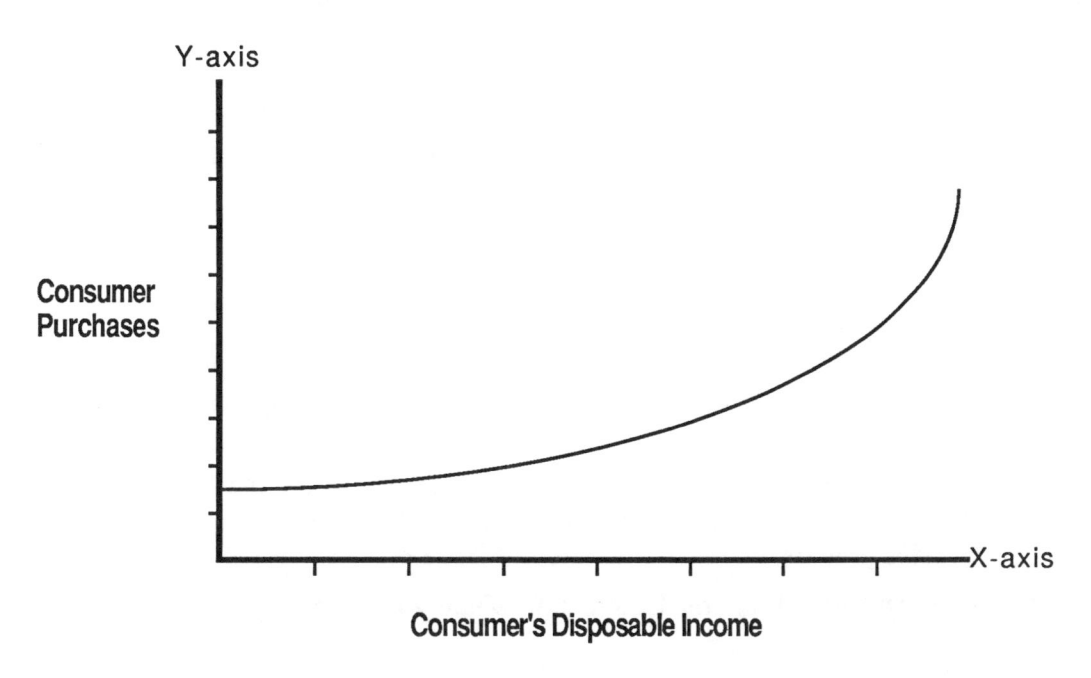

**3. Minimum grid lines.** Keep grid lines to a minimum on your graph in order to highlight the data, not the background. Too many lines can reduce a graph's legibility and lessen its impact.

**4. Standard graph paper.** Sticking to commercially produced graph paper will your job easier, as well as that of the professional draftsman (if one is used). It eliminates the job of redrawing curves to a new scale and minimizes the chance of error.

**5. Line weight that emphasizes curve.** If grid marks cannot be entirely eliminated, then make sure that they are lighter than the graph line(s). Also, it may be desirable to emphasize certain divisions on the scale (such as a slightly heavier line at every increment of 50 on a scale of 0-300), to improve readability.

Make the major graphed lines about six times heavier than the lightest grid line, and secondary lines at least three times the weight of the lightest grid mark.

**6. Content: clear, uncluttered.** The title goes below the graph, outside the grid and axes. Place the figure number before the title. Supporting material should be kept to a minimum and well separated from the graph. When labeling the axes, put the unit of measurement (hours, years, grams, inches or whatever) in parentheses after the title: "Output (gallons/hour)."

Limit the number of lines on a black-and-white graph to four or five. Color can afford you a few more, but be sure the result isn't overcrowded or confusing. Consider tracing-paper overlays when the number of lines gets out of hand.

Labeling of lines and everything on the graph should be done by typewriter or stencil. Hand-written letters give it an unprofessional look and therefore detract from its credibility and impact. Show the reader that you thought enough of your work to present it perfectly.

## Illustrations

Illustrations, whether they are photographs or drawings, will be used infrequently in management reports. When choosing between these two forms of illustration, go for the one that demonstrates your point with the greatest impact. Of course the expense of obtaining and reproducing photographs will be a factor, but try to weigh the costs involved against how much they would add to the report.

When dealing with photographic illustrations, be sure to:

1. Thoroughly discuss with the photographer what you want the photo to achieve. If you can, go with him to the "shoot" to make sure he is capturing what you are looking for.

2. Have all extraneous background and details removed from the shot. Those that cannot be physically removed or masked will have to be airbrushed out—an expensive process.

3. Crop the photo to focus reader attention where you want it.

4. Illustrate the scale of the photo by having a familiar object or ruler in the picture if there is likely to be any confusion in interpreting it.

5. Have the photos printed as part of the report if at all possible. Inserting glossies makes the report bulky and inconvenient to handle, and the photos frequently come unmounted.

6. Caption each photo and explain it clearly when the photo is not self-explanatory.

Most of the photographic guidelines also apply to drawings. In addition, consider these items when dealing with drawings:

1. Have a professional do the drawings, and coach him on what you want before he begins.

2. Go for simplest rendition that will illustrate your point.

3. Follow all the guidelines mentioned above in items #4, #5, #6 under "Illustrations."

# Appendix VI

# Similar Words

The English language is replete with words that are so similar in sound or spelling (or both) that they are easily confused, even by careful writers. The list below will acquaint you with some of these. Pay particular attention to pairs of words with different "shades" of meaning, as in "admission" and "admittance." This list does not include words that merely have two acceptable spellings.

| | | | |
|---|---|---|---|
| abjure | To reject; to renounce under oath | averse to | Having a strong feeling of opposition to |
| adjure | To command or request earnestly | advice | Opinion, counsel, or recommendation (noun) |
| ad | An informal expression or abbreviation for "advertisement" (an ad in the newspaper) or "advertising" (an ad executive) | advise | To give counsel, to offer an opinion, to recommend (verb) |
| | | agenda | A list or outline of things to be done |
| add | To join or unite so as to increase in number, size, or scope | addenda | Something to be added; supplements to a book (singular: addendum) |
| adapt | To adjust or modify for a new use; to make suitable | aid | To provide help or assistance; someone who acts as a helper |
| adept | Highly skilled, proficient, expert | aide | A military official who acts as an assistant to a superior, an aide-de-camp |
| adopt | To take or accept as one's own | | |
| admission | Both of these words refer to the act of admitting or permission to enter, but "admittance" usually applies to physical entry to a specific place ("Admittance to the operating room was forbidden"), while "admission" connotes a right or privilege of participation ("admission to the club," or "the high price of admission") | allocate | To set aside for a particular purpose |
| | | locate | To set or determine the place of |
| admittance | | location | A position or site occupied |
| | | locution | A particular style of expression or unique way of phrasing things |
| | | allocution | A formal speech |
| | | allusion | A passing reference to something, either directly or by implication, as in "a literary allusion" |
| adverse | Hostile, contrary, or opposed to one's interests | delusion | A false belief |
| | | elusion | Evasion or escape |

137

| | | | | |
|---|---|---|---|---|
| illusion | A misapprehension; a misleading image | | ante- | A prefix meaning prior or before, as in "antebellum"—before the Civil War |
| allay | To calm, to subdue | | anti- | A prefix meaning opposed or hostile to, as in "antiwar" |
| alley | A narrow street or enclosed garden walk | | | |
| ally | To formally unite (verb); a supporter or associate (noun) | | antedate | To assign a date prior to that of actual occurrence |
| | | | postdate | To assign to a date after actual occurrence |
| aloud | Vocally | | | |
| allowed | Granted or permitted | | antidote | A remedy |
| out loud | Loudly enough to be heard; aloud | | anecdote | A short narrative or brief story |
| already | Previously; by this time | | antiseptic | Scrupulously clean; destroying bacteria |
| all ready | In readiness | | anesthetic | Lacking awareness; producing insensibility |
| altar | A raised structure; a place that serves as a center of worship | | aseptic | Free of germs |
| alter | To make different | | anyhow | At all; by any means |
| alternate | To perform by turns (verb); a substitute (noun) | | anyway | In any manner whatsoever; in any event; anyhow |
| alternative | Offering a choice (adjective); an opportunity to choose between two or more things (noun) | | any way | In any way or manner. When talking about course or direction, use "any way," as in "Any way we choose to go will endanger us." |
| although though | "Although" and "though" may be used interchageably, but if it comes first, "although" is preferred ("Although he was young, he ran for senator" vs. "He ran for senator, though very young.") "Though" is often used to link single words or phrases, as in "younger though more experienced." | | a piece | By the piece, as in "a shipping charge of $.50 a piece" |
| | | | apiece | Each or for each person or thing, as in, "We ate three apples apiece." |
| | | | appertain | To relate to, to belong to |
| | | | pertain | To belong to, less formal than "appertain" |
| tho | "Though" (informal and unacceptable in formal writing) | | appurtenance | Something added to or belonging to a more important thing; an adjunct or accessory |
| altogether | Entirely, completely ("You're altogether wrong about him") | | pertinent | Significant to or related to the matter at hand |
| all together | Collectively, in the sense of unity ("The winners stood all together at one end of the stage") | | appraise | To estimate the quality, size, weight, or worth of |
| | | | apprise | To notify or inform |
| analyst | A person who analyzes | | apprize | To value |
| annalist | An historian, a writer of annals | | | |
| angel | A spiritual being | | ark | A place of refuge or security |
| angle | A corner or viewpoint | | arc | An unbroken part of the circumference of a circle; a curved line |
| annihilator | Someone who nullifies or destroys | | arrange | To place in the proper or desired order |
| nihilist | Someone who believes that nothing exists, is known, or can be communicated | | arraign | To accuse or charge; to bring before a court of law |

| | |
|---|---|
| ascetic | Abstinent; austere (an "ascetic" lifestyle) |
| acetic | Pertaining to, producing, or derived from acetic acid, as in vinegar |
| aesthetic | Having a love of beauty or a sense of the beautiful |
| assay | To try or put to the test |
| essay | A short prose composition on a particular theme |
| assembly | An organized gathering of a group of people for a particular purpose |
| assemblage | A collection; a number of persons or things assembled |
| assent | To give in, to yield |
| ascent | A rising movement, the act of ascending |
| accent | Prominence of a syllable within a word; a mark indicating stress; a foreign accent |
| astray | Off the right path or route; straying |
| stray | A person, animal or thing that wanders or is lost |
| auger | A tool for boring |
| augur | A prophet (noun); to predict or foreshadow (verb) |
| aught | Anything whatsoever; in any degree |
| ought | An auxiliary verb used to express obligation or expectation ("We really ought to go see her") |
| away | Far or apart; from this or that place, as in "Go away" |
| aweigh | A nautical term meaning lifted from the bottom, as in "Anchors aweigh!" |
| way | A course or route; distance or direction (Note the difference between "Give way"—meaning to submit—and "Give away.") |
| awhile | For a short period of time (adverb); as in, "Why don't you stay awhile?" |
| a while | Usually part of a prepositional phrase, used with "for"; as in, "Why don't you stay for a little while?" |
| backup | Something that serves as a substitue or alternative; in relation to computers, a duplicate copy |
| back up | To move to a position behind; to accumulate |
| basic | Fundamental |
| BASIC | A computer programming language (acronym for Beginners All-purpose Symbolic Instruction Code) |
| bad | Unsound, unfavorable, poor |
| bade | Past tense of "bid," meaning to request or invite (pronounced bad) |
| bail | To empty water from a boat; to parachute from a plane, as in "bail out" |
| bale | A large bundle of goods |
| bait | To tease, lure, or harass |
| bate | To restrain or reduce the intensity of something ("with bated breath") |
| bald | Lacking in hair or other natural covering |
| balled | Past tense of "ball," meaning to form or gather into a ball |
| bawled | Past tense of "bawl," meaning to cry out loudly |
| ballet | A classical dance form |
| ballot | A slip of paper on which a voter marks his choice |
| baneful | Destructive; harmful |
| baleful | Ominous, menacing |
| barbaric | Primitive; uncivilized |
| barbarous | Wild, savage, crude |
| barbarian | An unrefined, uncultured, uncivilized person |
| baron | A low-grade nobleman |
| barren | Sterile, unproductive |
| base | A bottom support, usually applied to material things (noun); morally low or without dignity (adjective) |
| bass | Low in pitch |
| basis | The groundwork, the fundamental principle or ingredient (usually used in a nonphysical sense) |

| | | | |
|---|---|---|---|
| bathos | An abrupt transition from the sublime to the ordinary; an anticlimax | board | A piece of sawed lumber; daily meals; an organized group |
| pathos | A quality that arouses pity or sympathetic feelings | bored | Wearied, restless |
| | | boarder | A lodger |
| bazaar | A market place | border | An edge or boundar |
| bizarre | Whimsically strange, unusual in appearance or style | bolder | More bold (fearless) |
| | | boulder | A large stone |
| beat | To strike repeatedly; to overcome or defeat | born | Brought forth |
| beet | A garden vegetable with an edible root | borne | Past tense of "bear," meaning to endure |
| | | bourn | A stream or brook |
| bellow | To make a loud sound (like a bull) | bow | Something bent into a curve; a weapon used in archery; a knot with two or more loops; a violin bow (pronounced boh) |
| below | In a lower place; beneath | | |
| billow | To swell; to rise or roll in waves | bow | To bend the head in reverence or salutation (verb); the forward part of a ship (noun) (pronounced bau) |
| berry | A small, edible fruit | | |
| bury | To cover with earth | | |
| berth | Place where a ship lies at anchor; space to maneuver | bough | A tree branch (pronounced bau) |
| | | beau | A boyfriend (pronounced boh) |
| birth | Beginning or start; the emergence of new life | boy | A male child |
| | | buoy | A floating signal (nautical term) |
| beside | By the side of; in comparison with; not relevant to ("beside the point") | breach | A gap; a violation; a severance |
| | | breech | The lower part |
| besides | Except; moreover; other than ("Besides that, he was right") | break | To smash or reduce to pieces (verb); an opening or act of disruption (noun) |
| biannual | Occurring twice a year | brake | A device for slowing or stopping a moving vehicle |
| biennial | Occurring every two years | | |
| | | breath | Respiration; a pause; a slight stirring of air |
| bit | In computer technology, a single, basic unit of information; a small piece | breathe | To take in air (verb) |
| | | breadth | Width |
| bite | To seize with the teeth; to eat into | bridal | Pertaining to a wedding |
| | | bridle | Part of a horse's harness; something that restrains |
| byte | With reference to computers, a unit of information equal to one character (or eight bits) | broach | To mention or suggest for the first time (as in, "to broach a subject") |
| bloc | A coalition of parties or factions ("the Eastern bloc") | brooch | A clasp or ornamental pin |
| block | A solid piece of wood; a cube-shaped piece | bullion | Gold or silver in the form of ingots |
| | | bouillon | A clear broth |
| boar | A male swine | | |
| bore | To make a hole (verb); a tiresome person (noun) | burrow | A shelter or hole in the ground made by an animal |
| boor | A peasant | burro | A small donkey |
| Boer | A South African of Dutch descent, as in "the Boer War" | borough | A municipality smaller than a city |

| | | | |
|---|---|---|---|
| by | A preposition ("by the way") | casual | Offhanded, happening by chance |
| buy | To acquire through purchase | | |
| bye | Secondary, out of the way ("by the bye") | causal | Constituting or implying a cause |
| | | causality | The relation of cause and effect |
| cagey | Shrewd, cautious | | |
| cadging | Begging or borrowing without intent to repay | censor | A person who supervises the morality of others (noun); to delete an objectionable word or phrase from a text (verb) |
| calendar | A system of reckoning time, a chronological list | | |
| | | censure | A strong expression of condemnation or disapproval (noun); to criticize or blame (verb) (pronounced sencher) |
| calender | A machine that presses cloth or paper for glazing, etc. | | |
| colander | A metal or plastic sieve or strainer | | |
| | | censer | A container for burning incense |
| callous | Hardened, thickened; without emotion (adjective) | ceremonial | Formal, ritual |
| | | ceremonious | Pertaining to or characterized by ceremony |
| callus | A thickening of the skin (noun) | | |
| cannon | A piece of artillery | chafe | To warm by rubbing; to irritate |
| canon | A regulation decreed by a church; an accepted principle or rule | chaff | The husks of grains; worthless matter |
| | | champaign | Level, open country |
| canyon | A deep, narrow valley | champagne | A sparkling white wine |
| | | campaign | A connected series of operations, usually military or political |
| cannot | The common spelling for "can not" | | |
| can not | Used for emphasis, as in "It's not that he will not—he can not speak") | | |
| | | chased | Past tense of "chase," meaning pursue |
| canvas | A heavy, closely woven cloth | chaste | Virtuous, pure, stainless |
| canvass | To examine in detail, as in "to canvass votes" | | |
| | | cheap | Inexpensive |
| | | cheep | To chirp or peep |
| capital | The top of a column; punishable by death; accumulated goods; a capital letter | childish | Weak, silly; like or befitting a child |
| | | childlike | Like a child in innocence or frankness |
| Capitol | (capitalized) The building in Washington, D.C. that houses the Congress; if not capitalized, a statehouse | | |
| | | chord | Three or more musical notes played at the same time |
| | | cord | A long, slender, flexible material consisting of several strands wound together; a unit of wood |
| carat | A unit of weight for precious stones | | |
| caret | A proofreading symbol | | |
| carrot | A vegetable | | |
| karat | A measure for gold | | |
| cache | A hiding place | clamor | A loud noise or uproar |
| cachet | Indication of approval; a feature or quality that confers prestige | clamber | To climb with effort or difficulty |
| cash | Ready money | | |
| cast | To throw or direct; a throw of dice; a group of actors | clause | A group of words containing a subject and predicate which form a part of a sentence |
| caste | An hereditary social class (as in Hinduism) | | |
| | | claws | The sharp nails of an animal |

141

| | |
|---|---|
| click | A slight, sharp sound |
| cliche | A trite expression (pronounced kleeshay) |
| clique | A small, exclusive social group (pronounced kleek or klik) |
| claque | A group of people hired to applaud (pronounced klak) |
| climatic | Pertaining to climate |
| climactic | Pertaining to a climax |
| climacteric | A critical period of time |
| clinch | To secure, fasten, or settle |
| clench | To grip or close tightly |
| clothes | Garments, wearing apparel |
| close | To shut; to finish or conclude |
| cloths | Pieces of fabric (pronounced klawths) |
| coarse | Of inferior quality; lacking in refinement |
| course | Progress; route or path taken; a part of a meal; a unit of a curriculum |
| coin | A small piece of metal used as money (noun); to invent a word or phrase (verb) |
| quoin | An exterior angle of a wall; a cornerstone |
| coign | As in the phrase, "coign of vantage," meaning an advantageous position |
| collision | A crash; a conflict of ideas or interests |
| collusion | A secret agreement; a conspiracy |
| coma | A state of prolonged unconsciousness |
| comma | A punctuation mark used to indicate a pause |
| comic | Pertaining to comedy; amusing |
| comical | Provoking laughter, as in "She had a comical way of expressing herself." |
| complacent | Contented, self-satisfied |
| complaisant | Showing a desire to please; obliging |
| complement | Something that completes or brings to perfection |
| compliment | An expression of admiration |
| compose | To make or create; to settle |
| comprise | To consist of; to include |
| comprehensible | Capable of being understood; intelligible |
| comprehensive | Large in scope or content, inclusive |
| compute | To determine by mathematical means |
| commute | To travel back and forth regularly; to substitute or exchange |
| condemn | To criticize, pronounce judgment against |
| contemn | To despise |
| confidant | One to whom secrets are confided |
| confident | Self-assured |
| confidently | With self-assurance |
| confidentially | Communicated in secret |
| congenial | Agreeable; having the same tastes or interests |
| genial | Cordial, kindly; conducive to life or growth |
| congenital | Inherent; existing from birth |
| conjurer | A wizard or magician; someone who entreats or appeals to someone (also spelled conjuror, with accent on first syllable) |
| conjuror | One who is bound by an oath taken with others (accent on second syllable) |
| contagious | Communicable by contact, as in a "contagious disease" |
| infectious | Capable of being transmitted without actual contact; causing infection |
| contemptible | Worthy of contempt or scorn |
| contemptuous | Manifesting, feeling, or expressing contempt |
| continual | Continuing indefinitely without interruption, but usually in the sense of "repeated at intervals," as in "the continual banging of the door in the storm" |
| continuous | Unceasing; without interruption in time or unbroken in space, as in "a continuous vigil throughout his illness" |
| continuing | Existing over a prolonged period of time; needing no renewal |

| | |
|---|---|
| constant | Persistent, unchanging |
| continuance | Duration; an adjournment of court proceedings until the following day |
| continuation | The prolongation of an activity; the resumption of an activity after interruption |
| coo | To make a sound like a dove or pigeon |
| coup | A sudden, brilliant, and often succesful act, as in "coup d'etat" (pronounced koo) |
| coop | A cage for poultry (noun); to confine (verb), as in "coop up" |
| coral | The skeletal deposit produced by a small sea animal |
| corral | An enclosure for livestock |
| choral | Of or relating to a chorus or choir |
| chorale | A hymn or psalm; a choir |
| core | The innermost part |
| corps | A body of persons acting together, especially in a military sense (pronounced kor) |
| corpse | A dead body |
| corporal | An infantry soldier who ranks just above a private |
| corporeal | Pertaining to the body; tangible |
| correspondent | One who communicates by writing |
| corespondent | A person charged with adultery with the defendant in a divorce suit |
| corrosion | The process of dissolving or wearing away |
| erosion | The wearing away by action of water, wind, or glacial ice |
| council | A group of people called together for consultation or deliberation |
| counsel | Advice or guidance; an exchange of ideas |
| consul | A person appointed by a government to live in a foreign city and look after the country's interests |
| courtesy | Polite behavior; a favor |
| curtsy | A gesture of respect, usually made by women |
| creak | A grating or squeaking sound |
| creek | A small stream |
| crick | A muscle spasm or cramp |
| credible | Believable, plausible |
| creditable | Deserving of credit or commendation |
| credulous | Gullible, easily deceived |
| credit | To believe, trust, or give credit to |
| accredit | To ascribe credit to, to authorize |
| crevice | A fissure, cleft, or narrow opening |
| crevasse | A deep fissure, as in a glacier |
| critic | One who expresses judgment |
| critique | A critical review or discussion |
| crumble | To disintegrate or fall into ruin |
| crumple | To crush out of shape |
| cue | A hint or signal |
| queue | A line of people; a long braid of hair |
| currant | A small seedless raisin |
| current | Occurring or existing in the present time (adjective); the swiftest moving part of a body of water (noun) |
| days | The plural form of "day" |
| daze | To stupefy, stun, or dazzle with light |
| decant | To pour a liquid (such as wine) from one container to another |
| descant | An ornamental melody played above a musical theme (noun); to discourse, to sing melodiously (verb) |
| decease | Death |
| disease | An illness or abnormal condition |
| demise | Death; the transfer of a ruler's authority by death |
| decent | Adequate, respectable, tolerable |
| descent | A coming or going down |
| dissent | Difference of opinion, disagreement |
| decree | An order having the force of law |
| degree | The extent of an action; an academic title conferred on the graduates of a university or college |

| | | | |
|---|---|---|---|
| decry | To express strong disapproval of; to discredit | disassemble | To take apart |
| descry | To catch sight of, to see something in the distance | dissemble | To disguise, hide, or feign |
| | | disburse | To pay out |
| definite | Free of ambiguity or uncertainty | disperse | To scatter or spread widely |
| definitive | Authoritative, conclusive | discomfit | To frustrate, thwart, or put into a state of embarrassment |
| demean | To debase or humble oneself | discomfort | To make uncomfortable or uneasy |
| demesne | Legal possession of land (pronounced dimane) | discreet | Prudent; showing good judgment |
| depositary | A person entrusted with the safekeeping of something | discrete | Consisting of individual or distinct elements; separate |
| depository | A place of safekeeping | | |
| deprecate | To belittle or express disapproval of | disinterested | Impartial, unbiased |
| depreciate | To lessen the value of | uninterested | Not paying attention; unconcerned |
| desecrate | To profane or abuse the sacredness of | dispense | To deal out or distribute |
| | | dispense with | To forgo or dispose of |
| descendant | A person descended from others | disprove | To prove to be false or invalid |
| descendent | Moving downward, descending (adjective) | disapprove | To have an unfavorable opinion of |
| desert | A barren region marked by low rainfall (noun); to forsake, leave or abandon (verb) | disseminate | To scatter widely, to disperse |
| | | dissimulate | To disguise or conceal |
| deserts | That which is deserved, as in, "his just deserts" | distinct | Individual, not similar |
| dessert | A sweet dish; the last course of a meal | distinctive | Characteristic, serving to identify |
| | | distrait | Absentminded, distracted because of anxiety |
| deserve | To merit or be worthy of | distraught | Anxious, worried, distracted |
| disserve | To treat badly, to do a disservice to | distraint | A legal term meaning the act or process of seizing property to force payment of debts |
| desirable | Arousing desire, pleasing | | |
| desirous | Characterized by desiring | divers | Various, sundry |
| detract | To diminish or take away something | diverse | Different, unlike |
| distract | To sidetrack or divert | done | Past tense of "do"; finished; cooked adequately |
| device | Something constructed for a particular purpose (noun) | dun | To demand payment |
| devise | To arrange in the mind, to plan | dose | A specified quantity |
| | | doze | To sleep lightly, to nap |
| Dictaphone | A phonographic device that records and reproduces dictation for transcription | draft | A current of air; a gulp; conscription for military service; the act of drawing |
| dictograph | A telephonic instrument that reproduces sounds from a transmitter by means of a small microphone | drought | A long period of time without rain (pronounced draut) |
| die | To cease living | dual | Composed of two parts |
| dye | A substance used to color or stain | duel | A struggle or combat between two persons |

144

| | | | |
|---|---|---|---|
| dungeon | A dark chamber for prisoners | empire | A political unit covering a large territory |
| dudgeon | A sullen, angry or indignant mood | umpire | A judge or arbiter; one who settles disputes, as in a baseball game |
| dying | In the process of succumbing to death | ended | Used to indicate time past, as in "The week ended on the second of June" |
| dyeing | Being stained or colored | | |
| dieing | Being cut, formed, or stamped with a die | ending | Used to indicate present or future time, as in "I'll see you sometime during the week ending June 2" |
| earn | To receive for services; to get as a consequence | | |
| urn | An ornamental vase | endorse | To write one's name on the back of a check; to express approval of |
| earthly | Of this world (as opposed to spiritual or heavenly) | indorse | To endorse, often used in a legal context |
| earthy | Pertaining to or consisting of earth | energize | To activate, give energy to |
| effete | Barren; no longer capable of production; worn out | enervate | To weaken; to make feeble |
| au fait | Skilled; accomplished | innervate | To stimulate to movement or action |
| egoism | A tendency to be self-centered or conceited | innovate | To do something in a new way |
| egotism | Excessive reference to oneself in speaking or writing | enormity | The condition of being monstrous, outrageous, or wicked, as in "the enormity of the crime" |
| eldest | The first-born in a family | | |
| oldest | The most advanced in age (when referring to other persons or things) | enormousness | The state of being huge or excessive |
| | | entomology | The study of insects |
| elemental | Basic or powerful; of or like the four elements (earth, air, water, fire) | etymology | The study of the origins of words |
| | | envelop | To cover, surround, wrap up (verb) (accent second syllable) |
| elementary | Introductory, fundamental, basic; simple | envelope | A wrapper or covering, usually for correspondence (noun) |
| eligible | Fit to be chosen | | |
| legible | Readable, easily deciphered | epic | Heroic, majestic, imposing (adjective); a long narrative poem (noun) |
| illegible | Impossible or difficult to read | | |
| emerge | To rise out of; to come forth | epoch | The beginning of a new important period in the history of something; an extended period of time |
| immerge | To plunge into or under a fluid | | |
| emigrate | To leave one's country or place of residence to live elsewhere | | |
| immigrate | To come into a country of which one is not a native | epigram | A terse, witty statement |
| | | epitaph | An inscription on a tomb or monument |
| migrate | To move from one country or place to another | epithet | An appropriately descriptive word or phrase |
| emollient | Something that soothes or softens | equable | Characterized by evenness or uniformity |
| emolument | Compensation; the returns one gets from holding office or employment | equitable | Impartial; possessing or exhibiting equity |

145

| | | | |
|---|---|---|---|
| erasable | Capable of being erased | exodus | A journeying forth (usually on a large scale) |
| irascible | Irritable, easily angered | | |
| err | To blunder, to be mistaken or wrong | exotic | Foreign; strangely beautiful |
| | | exoteric | External, understood by the general public |
| ere | Before, sooner than | | |
| e'er | Ever (a contraction) | esoteric | Understood only by a select group |
| errant | Wandering, roving, rambling | expatiate | To roam; to enlarge or elaborate |
| arrant | Without moderation, extreme; notorious | expiate | To atone for |
| eruption | A breaking or bursting forth, as in "a volcanic eruption | expedient | Useful for bringing about a desired result; personally advantageous |
| irruption | A bursting in; a swift invasion | expeditious | Prompt, efficient, speedy |
| euphemism | A phrase that substitutes for one that is considered offensive or distasteful | extant | Still existing |
| | | extent | Length, breadth, or scope |
| euphuism | An artificial, high-flown style of speech or writing | extinct | No longer existing; having no living descendant |
| exalt | To elevate, to lift up | extract | A passage taken from a writing (usually large) |
| exult | To rejoice | excerpt | A passage selected or quoted (usually small) |
| exceed | To go too far; to surpass | | |
| accede | To express approval or give consent | facet | Any of the small, polished surfaces on a cut gem; a side or aspect |
| except | To exclude, to omit from consideration | facetious | Joking, especially at an inappropriate time |
| accept | To receive willingly; to endure | | |
| exceptional | Out of the ordinary; unusual, uncommon | factitious | Forced or artificial; not natural |
| | | factious | Causing dissension |
| exceptionable | Liable to exception or objection | fictitious | Imaginary, false; of or like fiction |
| excess | Above the usual or standard amount | fain | Gladly, readily |
| | | feign | To invent or imagine; to make a false show of |
| access | Permission or liberty to enter | | |
| excessive | Immoderate; characterized by excess | faint | To lose consciousness (verb); weak, feeble, exhausted (adjective) |
| exercise | To put into action; to use habitually | feint | A false show, a pretense; a deceptive movement |
| exorcise | To expel or cast out; to free from evil spirits | | |
| exhibit | To present or display (verb); a number of articles arranged for show (noun) | faker | One who fakes; a swindler or peddler |
| | | fakir | A Muslim beggar |
| exhibition | The act of exhibiting; a public show or display | farther | More remote, more distant |
| | | further | To a greater degree or extent |
| exposition | A large public exhibition, often international in scope; a detailed explanation or setting forth of facts | fatal | Inevitable; decisive; causing death or destruction |
| | | fateful | Prophetic; having important consequences |
| exit | A departure, a going out; a way out | | |

| | | | |
|---|---|---|---|
| fate | The force, principle or power that determines events; destiny | foggy | Misty, murky |
| fete | A festival or feast; an outdoor party | fogy | An old-fashioned person ("an old fogy") |
| | | follow | To come or go after; to accompany |
| faun | A rural deity in Roman mythology with the body of a man and the ears, horns, and legs of a goat | fallow | The plowing or tilling of land without sowing it for a season |
| fawn | A young deer (noun); to seek favor or attention (verb) | font | A bowl or basin for holy water; a source or origin |
| | | fount | A fountain or spring; a source of supply |
| faze | To disconcert or disrupt the composure of | forbear | To refrain from |
| phase | A stage in a series or cycle of changes | forebear | A forefather or ancestor |
| | | forbearance | Abstinence; tolerance or restraint |
| feet | Plural form of "foot" | | |
| feat | An extraordinary act of skill or daring | forceful | Effective, persuasive; full of force |
| | | forcible | Impressive; brought about by force |
| ferment | To produce by fermentation; to make turbulent or excite | | |
| foment | To promote the growth or arousal of; to instigate | forego | To go before in time, place, or degree |
| | | forgo | To do without, abstain from |
| fission | The act of splitting into parts | formally | In a formal manner |
| fusion | The act of melting together | formerly | Previously, in time past |
| flair | A natural talent or ability; a sense of what is stylish | fort | A fortified building |
| flare | To blaze up, to signal by flares; to curve outward | forte | The strong point; a special talent |
| flaunt | To make a showy or offensive display of | forward | At the front; advanced; ready or eager; bold |
| flout | To mock or treat with contempt | froward | Not willing to comply; adverse |
| flew | Past tense of "fly" | foul | Dirty, offensive, rotten; tangled or caught; an infringement of the rules of a game |
| flue | A pipe or shaft for the passage of smoke | | |
| flu | Colloquial expression for influenza | fowl | Any of the larger domestic birds, such as a chicken |
| flounder | To struggle awkwardly; to move in a stumbling manner; a fish | frays | Becomes worn or ragged |
| | | phrase | A group of words read or spoken as a unit |
| founder | To cause to fill with water and sink, as in "the ship foundered off the coast of Long Island" | freeze | To pass from a liquid to a solid state by loss of heat; to convert into ice; to immobilize |
| floe | A large flat field or sheet of moving ice | frieze | A decorative horizontal band |
| flow | To move as a fluid or in a stream | full | Containing all that is possible; complete |
| | | fulsome | Offensively excessive; loathsome |
| flower | A blossom; the best or finest part | | |
| flour | The fine ground meal of wheat or any other grain | funeral | The ceremony associated with the burial of the dead |

| | |
|---|---|
| funereal | Mournful; of or suitable to a funeral |
| fur | The thick, hairy covering of an animal |
| fir | A kind of tree, such as a pine |
| gamble | To play a game of chance; to take a risk |
| gambol | To leap about playfully; to frolic |
| gantlet | Variant of "gauntlet" |
| gauntlet | A glove, as in "to throw down the gauntlet" |
| gamut | The entire range or extent, as in "ran the gamut from the amateur to the professional" |
| gap | A hole or opening |
| gape | To stare open-mouthed |
| gate | An opening in a fence or wall; a structure that swings on hinges |
| gait | A manner of walking or running |
| genius | A person with a high intellectual endowment |
| genus | A classification of plants or animals |
| gentle | Of good birth; kindly; moderate |
| gentile | Not Jewish |
| genteel | Well-bred, refined, polite |
| gild | To overlay with gold |
| guild | An association for mutual aid; in Medieval times, a union of men in the same trade or craft |
| geld | To castrate a horse; to weaken |
| gilt | Gold or imitation gold laid on the surface of a thing |
| guilt | Culpability; a sense of wrongdoing |
| glazier | Someone who cuts and fits glass for windows |
| glacier | A huge mass of moving ice |
| goal | A purpose or objective |
| gaol | The British spelling of "jail" |
| gored | Pierced or stabbed; made with triangular pieces ("a gored skirt") |
| gourd | Any of various plants of the curcurbit family, including pumpkins, melons, squash, etc. |
| gorilla | A large ape |
| guerrilla | A member of a small defensive force that makes surprise raids behind enemy lines |
| gourmet | A connoisseur of fine food and drink |
| gourmand | A person who delights in eating well |
| great | Extremely large; eminent |
| grate | A grill or framework of bars (noun); to fragment or shred by rubbing; to annoy or irritate (verb) |
| grill | To broil; to question relentlessly |
| grille | A metal grating used as a screen or divider |
| grisly | Gruesome |
| grizzly | Grayish or flecked with gray; a bear |
| grove | A small stand of trees |
| groove | A long, narrow furrow or channel |
| guarantee | To assume responsibility for or vouch for (verb); something given or held as security (noun) |
| guaranty | A pledge; an agreement that secures the maintenance of something; something given or held as security |
| warranty | A guarantee or an assurance; an official authorization or sanction |
| hail | Precipitation in the form of ice pellets; to greet with approval |
| hale | Of sound health; robust |
| hair | The filaments that form the coat of an animal or cover the human scalp |
| hare | A kind of rabbit with long hind legs |
| hall | A corridor or passageway |
| haul | To pull or drag |
| hardy | Stalwart; capable of surviving unfavorable conditions |
| hearty | Exuberant; expressed with warmth of feeling |
| heartfelt | Earnest, sincerely felt |
| heal | To restore to health |
| heel | The posterior portion of the foot |

| | | | |
|---|---|---|---|
| healthful | Conducive to good health | human | Characteristic of man or mankind |
| healthy | Possessing good health | humane | Kind, merciful, compassionate |
| heard | Past tense of "hear" | hypercritical | Overly critical |
| herd | A group of cattle or other animals | hypocritical | Dissembling; displaying hypocrisy |
| hearsay | Rumor, report, common talk | ideal | Thought of as perfect |
| heresy | Beliefs or opinions at variance with established views | idle | Unoccupied, inactive |
| | | idol | An image of a god; an object of worship |
| heart | A muscular organ for pumping blood; the most vital part | idyll | A short poem or story describing a pastoral scene |
| hart | A stag | illicit | Prohibited; unlawful |
| hew | To cut or chop with an ax; to conform, as in "hew the line" | elicit | To bring out or draw forth |
| hue | Color or shade | imaginary | Existing only in the imagination; unreal |
| hie | To hasten | imaginative | Having a strong creative imagination |
| high | Tall, lofty, far above the ground | | |
| historic | Having importance or influence in history | imbue | To saturate or permeate |
| historical | Relating to or concerned with history | imbrue | To stain or saturate; to soak in blood |
| histrionic | Pertaining to actors; overemotional, dramatic | endue | To put on or cover; to provide with something |
| | | endow | To provide with a talent or quality; to bequeath money or property |
| hoard | A hidden supply | | |
| horde | A throng or swarm | | |
| hole | A cavity or opening | immersed | Plunged into a liquid; deeply engaged |
| whole | Complete, entire | | |
| holy | Revered; worthy of worship or esteem | emersed | Rising above the surface of the water |
| holey | Filled with holes | | |
| wholly | Completely, entirely, altogether | imminent | Impending; likely to happen at once, often threatening |
| holly | A tree or shrub used in Christmas decorations | immanent | Living or remaining within; inherent |
| homey | Having a feeling of home | | |
| homely | Domestic, familiar; plain, not pretty | eminent | Prominent; outstanding in performance or character |
| homily | A sermon | emanate | To come forth or proceed from |
| homogeneous | Uniform in structure or composition | immoral | Not conforming to accepted principles of right and wrong behavior |
| homogenous | Uniform in consistency; having a common origin | unmoral | Amoral; having no moral quality |
| | | amoral | Lacking moral judgment; not caring about right and wrong |
| hoop | A circular band of metal or wood | | |
| whoop | A shrill, prolonged cry | impassable | Not admitting passage ("an impassable road") |
| whop | To beat or thrash (verb); a heavy blow (noun) | impassible | Incapable of pain or suffering; apathetic, not revealing emotion |
| horse | A large hoofed animal | | |
| hoarse | Husky, croaking ("a hoarse voice") | impassive | Not feeling pain; invulnerable; unemotional; apathetic |

| | | | |
|---|---|---|---|
| imperial | Pertaining to an empire; having supreme authority | insensible | Practically imperceptible; unaware, unconscious |
| empirical | Relying upon observation or experiment | insensitive | Lacking sensitivity; unresponsive |
| empyreal | Pertaining to the sky; celestial | insight | The ability to understand the inner nature of things |
| imply | To suggest; to express indirectly | incite | To rouse, to stir up, to move to action |
| infer | To conclude from evidence; to deduce | insipient | Unwise, stupid |
| incarceration | Imprisonment, confinement | incipient | Just beginning to exist or appear |
| incarnation | Appearnace in human form | insoluble | Incapable of being dissolved |
| incidence | The extent or frequency of the occurrence of something | insolvable | Incapable of being solved |
| incidents | Events, occurrences | insolvent | Unable to meet debts; bankrupt |
| incipient | Just beginning to exist or appear | instance | A case or example |
| insipient | Unwise, stupid | instant | A moment |
| incredible | Unbelievable | insulate | To isolate; to prevent the passage of heat |
| incredulous | Disbelieving, skeptical | insolate | To expose to sunlight |
| indentation | The act of indenting; a notch or recess in the edge or border of something | insolent | Presumptuous, insulting |
| indention | The blank space between a margin and the beginning of an indented line, as in a paragraph | insure | To cover with insurance; to guarantee |
| | | ensure | To make sure of, to insure |
| | | assure | To give confidence to, to reassure |
| indigenous | Native; occurring naturally in an area | intelligent | Having intelligence; mentally acute |
| indigent | Poverty-stricken | intelligible | Comprehensible, understandable |
| indignant | Filled with anger aroused by something unjust | interpolate | To insert |
| | | interpellate | To question formally about government policy |
| indiscreet | Lacking discretion; imprudent | extrapolate | To estimate on the basis of known variables |
| indiscrete | Unified; not divided into separate parts | | |
| indict | To charge or accuse of a crime | interstate | Pertaining to or existing between two or more states |
| indite | To set down in writing | intrastate | Within the boundaries of a state |
| inapt | Not apt; not suitable | | |
| inept | Awkward, clumsy; inappropriate | inure | To accustom to something unfavorable by prolonged exposure or subjection |
| infect | To contaminate | | |
| infest | To overrun or inhabit in large numbers | immure | To enclose within walls; to confine |
| ingenious | Clever, resourceful | | |
| ingenuous | Candid, straightforward, naive, artless | isle | A small island |
| | | aisle | A narrow passageway or corridor |
| insensate | Lacking sensation, foolish, brutal | its | Possessive of "it" (no apostrophe) |
| insentient | Lacking perception, life or consciousness | it's | Contraction of "it is" |

|  |  |
|---|---|
| jam | To drive or wedge; to squeeze into a tight position (verb); a fruit preserve (noun); a predicament (noun) |
| jamb | The vertical posts of a door or window |
| jest | Something said to provoke laughter; a jeering remark |
| gist | The main point or idea |
| jibe | To be in accordance; to shift the sail from one side of the vessel to the other while sailing before the wind |
| gibe | To taunt, reproach, or scoff at |
| judicial | Pertaining to the administration of justice |
| judicious | Exhibiting sound judgment |
| junction | The act of joining; the place where two things meet |
| juncture | A crisis or turning point |
| kernel | A grain or seed |
| colonel | A military officer (pronounced kernl) |
| key | A means of control or entry; a device for opening a lock |
| quay | A wharf (pronounced kee) |
| laboratory | A room equipped for experimentation or research |
| lavatory | A washroom |
| lain | Past tense of "lie" |
| lane | A narrow country road |
| later | Subsequently |
| latter | More recent; the second of two or last to be referred to; near the end |
| lath | A thin strip of wood |
| lathe | A machine for shaping wood |
| leach | To remove the soluble contents of |
| leech | A bloodsucking worm; a parasite |
| leash | A chain, rope or strap attached to the collar of an animal |
| leaf | The green part of a plant or tree |
| lief | Readily, willingly |
| leave | To go out of or away from (verb); permission (noun) |
| lean | To incline or slant away from the vertical (verb); thin (adjective) |
| lien | A legal claim; the right to sell the property of a debtor to pay a debt |
| least | The lowest in importance; the smallest in magnitude or degree |
| leased | Past tense of "lease," meaning to rent |
| led | Past tense of "lead," meaning to guide |
| lead | A soft metallic element |
| legend | A popular story handed down from earlier times |
| legion | A multitude, large number |
| lesson | Something to be learned; a period of instruction |
| lessen | To decrease or minimize |
| levy | To impose or collect |
| levee | A raised embankment to prevent a river from overflowing |
| liable | Responsible; legally obligated; likely |
| libel | Any written statement that defames a person's character |
| liar | Someone who tells lies or falsifies |
| lyre | A musical instrument |
| lay | to put or place (something) |
| lie | To rest or recline; to deceive |
| lye | A substance obtained by leaching wood ashes |
| lifelong | Continuing for a lifetime |
| livelong | Complete, whole ("All the livelong day") |
| lightening | Making less heavy; relieving of cares |
| lightning | A natural electric discharge in the atmosphere |
| limb | A branch of a tree; an appendage of an animal (pronounced lim) |
| limn | To describe; to depict by drawing (pronounced lim) |
| lineal | Being in the direct line of descent from an ancestor |
| linear | Relating to or resembling a line |

| | |
|---|---|
| lineament | A distinctive line or contour, especially of the face |
| liniment | A medicinal ointment applied to the skin |
| links | Rings forming a chain |
| lynx | A large wild cat |
| literal | In accordance with the facts or the explicit meaning |
| littoral | pertainig to a shore or coastal region |
| livid | Extremely angry; discolored, ashen or pallid |
| lurid | Causing shock or horror; ghastly |
| load | A weight or mass; cargo |
| lode | A vein of mineral ore |
| loan | Anything lent for temporary use |
| lone | Single, solitary |
| loath | Reluctant, unwilling |
| loathe | To detest, abhor |
| local | Relating to a particular place; not broad or general |
| locale | A locality, with reference to some event; the scene or setting |
| lose | To mislay; to be unable to keep |
| loose | Unrestrained, slack |
| luxuriant | Fertile, lush, rich in growth |
| luxurious | Fond of or characterized by luxury |
| made | Past tense of "make" |
| maid | A domestic servant |
| magnet | A piece of iron or steel that has the power to attract iron or steel; a person or thing that attracts |
| magnate | An important or influential person |
| magnificent | Splendid, sumptuous, stately |
| munificent | Lavish, generous |
| main | Chief, principal |
| mane | Long, heavy hair growing from an animal's neck |
| manner | Kind, sort; custom, fashion; a way of acting |
| manor | The house of an estate; mansion |
| mantel | A shelf above the fireplace |
| mantle | A cloak or loose sleeveless garment |
| marine | Relating to the sea |
| maritime | Bordering on the sea; relating to commerce on the sea |
| marshal | An official (noun); to place in the proper order, rank, or position (verb) |
| martial | Relating to or suited to war or warriors |
| marital | Pertaining to marriage |
| martin | A small swallow-like bird |
| marten | A carnivorous mammal |
| mast | A long spar rising from the deck of a ship |
| massed | Assembled in large numbers |
| masterful | Competent; having the power and skill of a master |
| masterly | Executed with skill |
| mastery | Superiority; possession of great skill |
| material | The elements or substances from which something is or can be made |
| materiel | Equipment and supplies used by an organization |
| mean | To intend, to signify |
| mien | External appearance |
| meantime | Interval (usually a noun) |
| meanwhile | Intervening time (usually an adverb) |
| meat | Animal flesh; the edible portion of something |
| meet | To encounter |
| mete | To deal out or allot |
| medal | A piece of metal stamped with a design or an inscription |
| meddle | To interfere, to intrude in the affairs of others |
| meritorious | Deserving reward or notice |
| meretricious | Alluring by false, showy charms; tawdry |
| meticulous | Extremely careful |
| metal | A class of elements that conduct heat and electricity |
| mettle | Character or temperament |

| | |
|---|---|
| meter | An instrument for measuring |
| metier | Trade, calling, profession |
| miner | A person who works in a mine |
| minor | Lesser in size, number or amount; a person under legal age |
| missile | An object thrown or projected so as to strike a distant object |
| missive | A letter |
| missed | Past tense of "miss," meaning to fail to reach; to feel the absence of |
| mist | A vapor; something that dims or obscures; a fine spray |
| might | Power, bodily strength; past tense of may |
| mite | A small insect; a very little bit |
| militate | To have weight or effect |
| mitigate | To mollify, to alleviate |
| modal | Indicating or pertaining to a mode in grammar, in logic, or in music |
| model | An example or pattern; a person who displays clothing |
| mood | A state of mind or feeling; humor or temper |
| mode | Manner of existing or acting; the prevailing style or current fashion |
| moral | Pertaining to the distinction between right and wrong |
| morale | Condition; state of mind |
| morning | The early part of the day |
| mourning | The act of grieving |
| motive | Something that causes a person to act |
| motif | A recurring thematic element; a dominant idea |
| nap | A short sleep; a soft or fuzzy surface on something |
| nape | The back of the neck |
| naval | Pertaining to the navy |
| navel | The central point or middle; the mark on the abdomen where the umbilical cord was attached |
| necessities | Things that can't be done without |
| necessaries | Things indispensable to some purpose |
| need | To want or require |
| knead | To work into a mass |
| needed | Required, wanted |
| needful | Characterized by great need or distress |
| needy | Poverty-stricken |
| neglect | To disregard (verb); the act of neglecting (noun) |
| negligence | The habit of neglect |
| oar | A long piece of wood used for rowing |
| ore | A natural mineral deposit from which a metal can be extracted |
| o'er | A contraction for "over" |
| observance | The act of complying with a law or custom |
| obervation | The act of paying attention or noticing |
| official | One who holds an office or position; authoritative |
| officer | One who holds an office of authority or rank in a government, corporation, the military, etc. |
| officious | Excessively forward in offering one's advice or services; meddlesome |
| oral | Spoken rather than written; pertaining to the mouth |
| verbal | Pertaining to words |
| ordinance | An authoritative direction or command; a law |
| ordnance | Artillery |
| ordonnance | An arrangement of the parts in regard to the whole composition |
| Orient | The east; the countries of Asia |
| Occident | The west; the countries of Europe and the Western Hemisphere |
| orient | To cause to face the east; to discover the bearings of |
| orientate | To turn toward the east |
| overdo | To carry too far |
| overdue | Past due |
| packed | Past tense of "pack"; filled, wrapped tightly |
| pact | A formal agreement |

| | | | |
|---|---|---|---|
| pail | A bucket | personnel | The people employed by an organization or business; the staff |
| pale | Pallid, whitish in complexion; a stake or pointed stick; the area enclosed by a fence or boundary | personal | Private, one's own |
| pain | An unpleasant sensation; suffering; punishment | perspective | A view or vista; the appearance of objects in depth |
| pane | One of the divisions of a window or door | prospective | Looking forward in time; relating to the future |
| pair | Two corresponding persons or items | physic | A medicine, the art or science of healing diseases |
| pare | To remove the outer covering or skin of; to remove by cutting or clipping | psychic | Pertaining to the human mind |
| pear | A fruit | physique | The body ("a swimmer's physique") |
| palate | The roof of the mouth | plain | Clear, simple, uncomplicated |
| palette | A board on which an artist mixes colors; a range of colors | plane | A flat or level surface; a carpenter's tool; an airplane (noun); to rise out of the water, to soar or glide (verb) |
| pallet | A narrow, hard bed; a portable platform for handling materials | | |
| partake | To take a portion of; to have a share in | plaintiff | The party that institutes a legal suit |
| participate | To join or share with others | plaintive | Melancholy |
| partially | To a certain degree | plum | A kind of fruit |
| partly | In part, not completely | plumb | A lead weight hung at the end of a line (noun); to fall or sink straight down, to fathom (verb) |
| passed | Past tense of "pass," to move on or ahead | | |
| past | No longer current; bygone | | |
| peer | To look intently (verb); a person who has equal standing with another (noun) | pole | A long rod; either end of an axis; a point of reference |
| | | poll | A counting or voting |
| pier | A platform extending over water | poor | Having little or no wealth; inferior |
| percent | Per hundred | pour | To stream or flow; to rain hard |
| percentage | A fraction or ratio with 100 as the denominator; a proportion or share in relation to the whole | pore | To study carefully (verb); a minute orifice or opening (noun) |
| peremptory | Precluding further debate; expressing a command | populace | The common people |
| preemptive | Pertaining to the right to acquire something beforehand | populous | Densely populated; having many people |
| perpetrate | To be guilty of; to commit | portion | A part of a whole |
| perpetuate | To prolong the existence of | potion | A liquid dose of medicinal, magical or poisonous content |
| perquisite | A benefit in addition to a regular wage or salary | proportion | A part or share in relation to the whole |
| prerequisite | Required as a prior condition | | |
| persecute | To oppress or harass | practical | Designed for use, utilitarian; concerned with everyday activities |
| prosecute | To follow or pursue; to carry on a legal suit | practicable | Feasible; capable of being done |

| | | | |
|---|---|---|---|
| precede | To go or come before | proposal | A plan or scheme; an offer of marriage |
| proceed | To continue; to go forward or onward, especially after an interruption | proposition | An offer of terms for a transaction; the act of offering or suggesting something to be considered or adopted |
| precedence | Priority | | |
| precedents | Conventions or customs; acts that may be used as examples in dealing with similar future cases | provided | On the condition or understanding that |
| | | providing | On the condition (followed by "that")—but in most cases, the use of "provided" is preferred |
| precipitous | Extremely steep | | |
| precipitate | To hurl downward; to cause to happen before anticipated (verb); acting with excessive haste (adjective) | provisional | Providing or serving for the time being |
| | | provincial | Pertaining to the provinces; unsophisticated |
| precipitant | Impulsive; rushing or falling headlong; abrupt or unexpected | | |
| | | purpose | The reason for which something exists; an intended or desired result (noun) to set as an aim or intention (verb) |
| predicate | To affirm; to imply; the part of the sentence containing the main verb | | |
| predict | To make known in advance | propose | To offer or suggest for consideration |
| premier | First in status or importance; prime minister | | |
| premiere | The first public performance | rack | A framework on which things are hung |
| prescribe | To set down as a rule or guide; to recommend the use of | wrack | Damage or destruction; wreckage |
| proscribe | To denounce or condemn; to prohibit | rail | A horizontal bar of wood or metal (noun); to denounce or complain bitterly (verb) |
| presentiment | Previous conception; foreboding | railing | A fence-like barrier |
| presentment | The act of presenting a formal document to an authority | reality | The state or quality of being real; that which exists |
| presentation | A performance; a presenting | realty | Real estate |
| preview | To see before public showing | rebound | To spring or bounce back |
| purview | The scope of an act; the extent or range of control | redound | To have an effect or result; to accrue |
| principal | Most important; the chief person; the head of a school; a capital sum of money (noun and adjective) | receipt | A written acknowledgment of things received |
| | | recipe | A set of instructions for making something |
| principle | A fundamental truth or belief (noun) | recognizance | A bond or obligation entered before a court |
| profit | An advantageous gain or return | reconnaissance | A search for useful military information |
| prophet | One who foretells the future | | |
| prone | Lying face downward; having a natural inclination to something | recourse | A person or thing resorted to for help or protection |
| | | resource | A source of supply |
| supine | Lying face upward; inactive | reek | To smell strongly and unpleasantly |
| proportional | Pertaining to proportion; relative | wreak | To cause the infliction of vengeance or punishment |
| proportionate | In due proportion | | |

| | | | |
|---|---|---|---|
| refectory | A dining hall | shear | To cut; to clip the hair or fleece from |
| refractory | Difficult to manage | sheer | Transparently thin; unqualified; extending down or up steeply |
| reference | The act of conferring or consulting; consultation of sources of information; a statement on the qualifications of a person seeking employment | sight | Vision; something seen or worth seeing |
| | | site | A position or location |
| | | cite | To call upon; to quote; to name or refer to |
| referral | An act of referring; a recommendation to someone or for something | sleek | Smooth and glossy or slippery; well-fed or well-groomed; suave |
| | | slick | Smooth and glossy or slippery; clever, ingenious |
| regimen | A regulated course of diet, exercise, or manner of living | slight | Small in amount or degree; of little importance |
| regiment | A military unit | sleight | Skill, dexterity; A quick, deceptive movement ("sleight of hand") |
| respectfully | With politeness or deference | | |
| respectively | With respect to each in the order given | | |
| restful | Tranquil; giving rest | soluble | Capable of being dissolved |
| restive | Uneasy, impatient | solvable | Capable of being solved |
| restless | Perpetually agitated | | |
| raffle | A lottery | some | Of an unspecified number |
| riffle | To flip through quickly | sum | A total; the substance or gist |
| rifle | To ransack | | |
| salary | A fixed payment at regular intervals | some time | A period of time |
| | | sometime | At a time in the past; formerly |
| wages | Money paid on an hourly, daily, or piecework basis | sometimes | Now and then; occasionally |
| scrip | A receipt or certificate | sore | Painful, tender |
| script | Handwriting; the written text of a play, motion picture, etc. | soar | To rise or fly high into the air |
| | | spacious | Having ample room; extensive |
| | | specious | Plausible but not genuine |
| seize | To grasp; to take possession or control suddenly | special | Unusual, distinctive |
| cease | To stop; to discontinue | especial | Outstanding, extraordinary |
| | | spatial | Relating to space |
| seller | A person who sells | | |
| cellar | A room below ground level used for storage | specially | In a special manner |
| | | especially | Particularly, markedly |
| sensible | Having or showing good sense; capable of being perceived by the senses | specialty | A special quality or feature; a thing specialized in |
| | | speciality | A distinctive mark or characteristic |
| sensitive | Readily affected; having acute emotional sensibility | | |
| serial | Anything published or broadcast in short installments at regular intervals | specie | Gold, silver and other coin, as opposed to paper money |
| | | species | A distinct kind or variety |
| cereal | An edible grain | | |
| session | A sitting together; an assembly of persons | statue | The form of a person or animal carved in wood, stone, etc. |
| | | statute | A law |
| cession | A yielding or surrender | stature | Height, development, elevation |
| secession | A withdrawal | | |
| cessation | A stopping | | |

| | | | |
|---|---|---|---|
| stimulant | Something that temporarily quickens a vital process; a food or beverage that stimulates | tasteful | Having, exhibiting, or conforming to good taste |
| stimulus | Something that incites to action; an incentive | tasty | Having an appetizing flavor |
| simulation | An imitation; the act of pretending | taught | Past tense of "teach" |
| | | taut | Tightly drawn; tense |
| straight | Without curves or angles; unbroken | team | A number of persons who perform an activity together |
| strait | A narrow strip of land with water on both sides; a narrow waterway | teem | To become filled to overflowing; to crowd |
| | | terminal | The end or extremity; a railroad terminal |
| subjugation | A bringing under control; conquering | terminus | A final goal or finishing point; either end of a transportation line |
| subjection | A forced endurance of something unpleasant or trying; subjugation | their | A possessive pronoun |
| | | there | In that place |
| suit | An appeal; a set of garments | they're | Contraction of "they are" |
| suite | A group of things forming a unit or constituting a collection | through | In one side and out the other; in the midst of; by way of |
| sweet | Pleasing to the taste; dear | threw | Past tense of "throw" |
| suspect | To imagine to be true or likely; to distrust | thorough | Exhaustive; painstaking |
| expect | To look for as likely to occur | throe | Pang, spasm; a hard or painful struggle |
| suppose | To hold as an opinion; to think probable | throw | To propel or fling |
| sustenance | A means of support or subsistence; food, provisions | tide | The rising and falling of the surface of the ocean |
| subsistence | The condition of remaining in existence; the means of subsisting | tied | Past tense of "tie" |
| | | toe | A part of the foot |
| | | tow | To draw or pull along behind |
| tantamount | Equivalent in value, significance or effect | tortuous | Marked by twists, bends or turns |
| paramount | Chief, supreme | | |
| temerity | Rashness, recklessness | torturous | Cruelly painful |
| timidity | Lack of courage or self-confidence | to | A preposition indicating movement toward, attachment or connection |
| tenant | Occupant; one who rents or leases | too | Also |
| tenet | A principle, belief, or doctrine | two | The number between one and three; a couple |
| tenor | The drift of something; a part in a chorus of voices | track | A series of marks left by the feet of a person or animal; a beaten path |
| tenure | A grasp or hold; status granted to a teacher | tract | A continuous expanse of land; a short treatise |
| tare | A deduction from the gross weight to allow for the weight of the container; a weed of grain fields | tack | A small, sharp-pointed nail (noun); to change course in a sailboat; to fasten in a hasty manner (verb) |
| tear | To pull apart by force, to rend; fluid secreted by a gland near the eye | | |

| | |
|---|---|
| transcribing | Present participle of "transcribe," meaning to copy or write down |
| transcription | An act of transcribing |
| transmission | The process of sending something; the passage of radio waves from one station to another |
| transmittal | A sending or conveying from one person or place to another |
| transmittance | The state of being transmitted |
| travel | The act of journeying to distant or unfamiliar places |
| travail | Toil, labor |
| triumphant | Victorious, conquering (pertaining to a person) |
| triumphal | Pertaining to the celebration of a victory or success |
| troop | A group of soldiers |
| troupe | A group of theatrical performers |
| trustee | One to whom something is entrusted |
| trusty | Dependable; a trusted convict with special privileges |
| turban | A headdress |
| turbine | A rotary engine |
| typical | Exhibiting the essential characteristics of a group |
| atypical | Not typical; irregular, unusual |
| typography | The style, arrangement or appearance of typeset matter |
| topography | The configuration of the surface |
| unabridged | Not shortened; complete |
| abridged | Condensed; shortened |
| expurgated | Cleansed of objectionable parts |
| underway | Occurring while in motion (adjective) |
| under way | In motion (adverb) |
| undo | To open or loosen; to reverse |
| undue | Not due; exceeding or violating propriety or fitness |
| undoubtedly | Without doubt |
| indubitably | Surely, unquestionably |
| unquestioned | Not questioned or disputed |
| unquestionable | Indisputable |
| urban | Relating to or characteristic of a city |
| urbane | Suave |
| usable | Capable of being used |
| useful | Serviceable; having utility |
| use | The employment or application of something |
| usage | A customary practice or procedure |
| vain | Idle, worthless; futile, unsuccessful; conceited, often about one's appearance |
| vane | A movable for showing the direction of the wind |
| vein | A blood vessel |
| vale | A valley |
| veil | A length of cloth used to cover the face; anything that obscures or conceals like a veil |
| valued | Past tense of "value"; esteemed |
| valuable | Having monetary value; having desirable characteristics |
| invaluable | Priceless, precious |
| venerable | Worthy of respect |
| vulnerable | Open to criticism or attack; capable of being hurt |
| vice | Moral depravity or weakness |
| vise | A tool for holding work |
| visa | An endorsement on a passport |
| viscous | Glutinous, syrupy |
| viscose | Made of viscose, an amber, syrup-like solution |
| viscosity | Resistance to flowing |
| vocation | Occupation; the work in which a person is regularly employed |
| avocation | A diversion; a hobby; a subordinate occupation |
| waist | The narrow central part of the body; the middle section |
| waste | A barren region, uncultivated land; damaged, rejected, or superfluous material |
| wait | To stay in expectation of |
| weight | The amount something weighs; a heavy object |
| want | A lack or absence; a craving |
| wont | Custom, habit |
| won't | Contraction of "will not" |
| wave | To sway to and fro; to signal with the hand |
| waive | To give up or forgo; to relinquish |

| | | | |
|---|---|---|---|
| waver | To vacillate or fluctuate; one who waves | wrangle | To quarrel or dispute angrily |
| waiver | A legal instrument abandoning a right or privilege | wangle | To manipulate; to bring about by persuasion |
| way | An opening; a course of action; an opportunity; a means; a path | wreck | To destroy or damage |
| | | wrack | To torture |
| weigh | To ascertain the heaviness of | wreak | To give vent to; to inflict (pronounced reek) |
| weak | Feeble; lacking strength | | |
| week | A period of seven days | your | The possessive of "you" |
| | | you're | Contraction of "you are" |
| wear | To have on; to use habitually; to waste gradually | yore | Time long past |
| ware | Merchandise (usually plural) | | |
| weir | A fence or enclosure in a waterway; a dam | who's | Contraction of "who is" |
| | | whose | The possessive of "who" |

# Appendix VII

# Colloquial Expressions

To say that a word or phrase is a "colloquialism" does not necessarily mean its usage is condemned. It does, however, mean it is an expression heard chiefly in conversation or used in informal writing. In other words, if you are writing a formal report or a business letter to someone you don't know very well and would like to impress, colloquialisms should be avoided.

The list below summarizes some of the most commonly used colloquial expressions. Those that appear with an asterisk (*) after them should be avoided in both writing and conversation.

| | |
|---|---|
| a | for "of." Don't say, "She's just that kind a* person." |
| ahold | for "hold." "Take ahold* of that rope for me, will you?" |
| all kinds of | for "many" or "much." "We've got all kinds of problems to worry about." |
| all the further or farther | for "as far as." Don't say, "That's all the further she got on all her own." |
| nowhere near | for "not nearly." |
| anywhere near | for "nearly." "He didn't make anywhere near the progress he'd hoped to." |
| around | for "about" or "near." "Around the first of the month." |
| as | for "that." "I don't see as* it's possible." |
| as like as not | for "likely." "As like as not* it will rain that day." |
| balance | for "rest" or "remainder;" "the balance of the year" except when referring to a financial balance, when it is permissible to say "the balance of your account." |
| bank on | for "rely on." "You can bank on our shipping it out to you next week." |

| | |
|---|---|
| because | for "the fact that." "Because* our service is faster is a good reason for using us." |
| blame it on | Don't say "She blamed it on herself" when you mean "She blamed herself." |
| broke | for "without money" or "bankrupt." "The business went broke last year." |
| can't seem | for "be unable." "That firm just can't seem to fill orders on time." |
| considerable | for "much." "You'll have considerable to gain if you join us." |
| contact | for "get in touch with." "I'll contact him firs." |
| don't ever | for "never." "Don't ever expect us to do that." |
| every bit | for "quite" or "in every way." "Our product is every bit as good as theirs." |
| expect | for "suppose." "I expect we'll be hearing from you before the month is out." |
| fine | for "well" or "much." "We hope you like it fine enough to call on us again." |
| first off | for "in the first place." "First off, we'd like to find out how much it costs." |
| folks | for "relatives" or "family members." "I guess you inherited the company from your folks." |
| funny | for "strange," "odd," or "puzzling." "Don't you think it's funny the package hasn't arrived yet?" |
| game | for "business." "She's in the health and fitness game." |
| going on | for "approaching" or "about." "It's going on five weeks since we heard from him." |
| got | for "was." "He got transferred." |
| guess | for "think," without uncertainty. "I guess we should go to that meeting now." |
| hear | for "have heard." "I hear they've got more work." |
| hear of | for "listen," or "consider." "He wouldn't hear of my going there alone." |
| in our midst | for "here," "with us," "among us," "in our city." |
| inside of | for "within." "They should be arriving inside of a week." |
| learn | for "have learned." "I learn from the accounting department that you haven't paid your bill yet." |
| leave | for "let." "Leave* him be" or "Leave* us face that fact that we're in trouble." |
| line | for "business" or "occupation," as in "Paper products aren't in his line." |
| locate | for "settle" or "become established." "They located somewhere on the west coast." |
| lose out | for "fail to succeed" or "be left out." "We might lose out on the deal if we wait." |
| lot | for "much" or "a great deal." "It would help us a lot if you'd try to meet your deadline." |
| mighty | for "very." "That was mighty thoughtful of them to take the extra time." |

| | |
|---|---|
| most | for "almost." "She spends most every day talking to her co-workers." While "most all the time" (meaning "almost all of") is colloquial, "most of the time" (meaning the largest part of") is naturally correct. TEST: Try "almost" first to see whether it sounds right. |
| mostly all | for "almost all" or "nearly all." "Our supply has mostly* all been used up." |
| on the side | for "besides" or "in addition." "He'll get a dividend and a bonus on the side." |
| outside of that | for "other than that," "besides that," or "except that." "Outside of the fact that we lost two managers...." |
| overly | for "too much" or "excessively." "He wasn't overly pleased to hear the news." |
| photo | for "photograph." |
| plenty good enough | for "sufficient" or "good enough." "A 15 percent raise is plenty good enough for me." |
| posted | for "informed." "We'll do our best to keep you posted." |
| price | for "ask the price of." "Price the alternatives and get back to us tomorrow." |
| proposition | for "business venture" or "project." |
| put in | for "spent" or "worked." "She put in almost 50 hours on that project last week." |
| read where | for "read that." "I read where they're selling the same thing for half the price." |
| real | for "very." "I think you'll find that our equipment works real well." ("Really" may be substituted, but it implies "actually" rather than "very." The best choice here would be "very.") |
| right | for "very." "We're coming along right well on the new building." |
| right along | for "repeatedly." "They'll call you right along in case you have problems." |
| run | for "manage," "Let's give him a chance to run this department on his own." |
| see | for "have seen." "I see by the date on this letter that you have a poor memory." |
| see where | for "see that." "I see where company profits increased 25 percent last year." |
| shape | for "condition." "The trucks are in good shape now." |
| some | for "somewhat" or "a little." "The new supervisor aggravated the situation some." |
| sooner | for "rather" or "just as soon." "I'd sooner work late tonight than come in early." |
| such a | for "so great a." "He's such a burden on the department that we may have to let him go." |
| sure | for "yes." "Sure" may properly be used for the adverb "surely," but should not be used in a slang manner to mean "certainly" or "indeed." "We sure would appreciate it." |

*Business Writing Made Simple*

| | |
|---|---|
| suspicion | for "suspect." "We didn't suspicion* that the deal would fall through." |
| take in | for "see." "We took in the trade show on our way home." |
| take sick | for "become ill." "If he hadn't take sick last week, the report would be done by now." |
| through | for "finished." "Will you be through by five o'clock?" |
| upwards of | for "more than." "We've got an order here for upwards of fifty pounds." |
| wait on | for "wait for." "He said he wouldn't wait on them all day; he wants to leave at 3:00." |
| way | for "away," "considerably," or "far." "These prices are way out of line for us." |
| win out | for "succeed." "The salesperson who wins out gets the account." |
| worst way | for "very much." "She wants that job in the worst way*." |
| write-up | for "article" or "press release." "I saw that write-up about your company in last night's paper." |

# Appendix VIII

# Latin Words and Phrases

| | |
|---|---|
| absente reo | the accused being absent |
| ad extremum | to the last, or extremity |
| ad finem | to the end |
| ad infinitum | to infinity |
| ad hoc | for this case only |
| ad hominem | to the man; to an individual's interests |
| adsum | I am present |
| ad nauseam | to satiety |
| ad referendum | for further consideration |
| ad valorem | according to the value |
| a fortiori | with stronger reason |
| alma mater | fostering mother; college attended |
| alter ego | another self |
| amicus curiae | friend of the court |
| anno Domini (A.D.) | in the year of our Lord |
| ante bellum | before the war |
| a priori | (reasoning) from cause to effect |
| aqua pura | pure water |
| aqua vitae | water of life; alcohol |
| aurora borealis | the northern lights |
| ave | hail |
| bona fide | with good faith or honesty |
| brevi manu | with a short hand; extemporaneously |
| carpe diem | enjoy the present day |
| casus belli | that which causes or justifies war |
| caveat emptor | let the buyer beware |
| cogito, ergo sum | I think, therefore I exist |
| conditio sine qua non | a necessary condition |
| corpus delicti | the body of the crime; the facts of the crime |
| crux | a cross; puzzle, difficulty |
| cum grano salis | with a grain of salt |

| | |
|---|---|
| cum laude | with praise or honor |
| de facto | in point of fact |
| de jure | from the law; by right |
| de novo | anew |
| de profundis | out of the depths |
| deus ex machina | a god out of a machine; a deity introduced to bring about the denouement of a drama |
| dramatis personae | the characters in a play |
| dulce et decorum est pro patria mori | It is sweet and glorious to die for one's country. |
| emeritus | retired with honor |
| e pluribus unum | one out of many; one composed of many |
| et alii, et aliae (et al.) | and others |
| et cetera (etc.) | and other things |
| ex cathedra | from high authority |
| excelsior | higher; loftier or taller |
| exempli gratia (e.g.) | for the sake of example |
| ex officio | by virtue of position |
| ex post facto | after the deed is done |
| ex voto | according to one's prayer or vow |
| facile princeps | easily preeminent; indisputably the first |
| fiat | let it be done; a sanction |
| flagrante delicto | during the actual commission of the crime |
| genius loci | the presiding spirit of a place |
| homo sui juris | a man who is his own master |
| horribile dictu | horrible to relate |
| ibidem (ibid.) | in the same place |
| id est (i.e.) | that is |
| in absentia | in the absence [of a person] |
| in camera | in judge's private office |
| in loco parentis | in place of a parent |
| in memoriam | in the memory of |
| in re | in the matter of |
| in situ | in the original place |
| in toto | wholly |
| ipso facto | by the fact itself |
| lapsus linguae | a slip of the tongue |
| lex loci | the law or custom of the place |
| loco citato (loc. cit.) | in the place cited |
| magna cum laude | with great praise or honor |
| magnum opus | a great work |
| mala fide | in bad faith |
| mea culpa | by my fault |
| mirabile dictu | wonderful to tell |
| modus operandi | manner of working |
| modus vivendi | mode of living |
| moraturi te salutamus | we who are about to die salute you |
| ne plus ultra | nothing further; the uttermost point |
| noli me tangere | touch me not |
| non sequitur | it does not follow |
| nota bene (N.B.) | note well |
| nulli secundus | second to none |
| omnia vincit amor | love conquers all |
| opere citato (op. cit.) | in the work cited |
| paterfamilias | male head of a household |
| per annum | by the year |
| per capita | by the head |
| per diem | by the day |
| per se | by or in itself |

### Appendix VIII–Latin Words and Phrases

| | |
|---|---|
| persona non grata | an unwelcome person |
| prima facie | on first sight |
| primus inter pares | first among equals |
| pro bono publico | for the public good |
| pro rata | in proportion |
| quid pro quo | one thing for another; tit for tat |
| rara avis | rare bird |
| re | in the matter of; in reference to the question of |
| reductio ad absurdum | reducing a proposition to absurdity |
| res judicata | a case or suit already settled |
| sanctum sanctorum | the holy of holies |
| semper fidelis | always faithful |
| sic | thus |
| sic transit gloria mundi | thus passes away the glory of the world |
| sine qua non | without which not  (an essential condition) |
| status quo | the state in which something is |
| sub rosa | under the rose; secretly |
| sui generis | of its own kind; in a class by itself |
| summa cum laude | with highest honors |
| tempus fugit | time flies |
| terra firma | solid ground |
| terra incognita | unknown ground |
| ultra vires | transcending authority |
| vale | farewell |
| via | by way of |
| vice versa | conversely |
| vincit amor patriae | the love of country prevails |
| viva voce | by the living voice |
| vox populi | the voice of the people |

# Appendix IX

# Superfluous Words

Business writing should never be cluttered with unnecessary words. But many of us use superfluous words every day without realizing it. Consider the following expressions; the words in bold are considered unnecessary.

| | |
|---|---|
| **ago** since | Do not say, "It is almost a year **ago** since we closed the deal." |
| alone...**only** | Use one word or the other, but not both. Don't say, "Is that **alone** your only reason?" |
| also...**too** | Again, use one word or the other. Do not say, "He also insists on that, **too**." |
| **and** etc. | This is obviously redundant. |
| assemble **together** | Also redundant. |
| **at** about | Do not say, "We're expecting you **at** about three o'clock." |
| attached **herewith** | "Herewith" is not only superfluous but wrong. "Hereto" would be more correct but is also unnecessary. |
| bars **out** | Do not say "This bars **out** the possibility that we'll be working together again." |
| both alike | "Both" is unnecessary if it is obvious that two are meant; otherwise "both" may be used. For example, "The employees are both alike in their qualifications." But do not say, "Both the company and its employees **alike** will benefit from the new plan." |
| both equally | If it is obvious that you're talking about two of something, "both" is superfluous; otherwise, "both equally" may be used. Say "The ideas were both equally ingenious," or "The two ideas were equally ingenious." |
| both together | "Both" is often superfluous in this combination. For example, it would be incorrect to say, "Were the two employees **both** together?" But sometimes "both together" is not only acceptable but necessary, as in "Hire one person or the other, but not both together." |
| but...**however** | One or the other is unnecessary. "We did not expect the package to arrive, but it was there on the doorstep **however**." |
| cancel **out** | "Cancel" implies "out"; therefore, "out" is usually redundant. |

*Business Writing Made Simple*

| | |
|---|---|
| consensus of opinion | The word "consensus" implies a collective opinion. But if you want to make this crystal clear, it may be added. There may also, of course, be a consensus of ideas, evidence, suggestions, etc. |
| contemplate **on** or **over** | Do not say, "They contemplated **on** filing for bankruptcy |
| continue **on** | Do not say, "We'll ask them to continue **on** with their work until the week is over." |
| **continue to** remain | Do not say, "If things **continue to** remain as they are, she'll have to be fired." |
| converted **over** | Do not say, "It was to be converted **over** into an auditorium." |
| **customary** practice | "Practice" implies a customary action. Do not say, "It is our **customary** practice to be fair with our customers." |
| depreciate **in value** | "Depreciate" usually means to decrease in value, but some things may depreciate in size or quality. Use "in value" only when it is needed for clarity. |
| each in its respective way | In most instances, the correct expression is "each in its way," or "respectively." |
| either...or **else** | Do not say, "They either accept our offer or **else** lose us as customers." |
| **else** but | Do not say, "We're not buying from anyone **else** but them." |
| enclosed **herewith** | This expression is used frequently, but "herewith" is superfluous. |
| endorse **on the back** | "Endorse" implies signing on the back of something, but not always. Only add "on the back" when it is absolutely necessary for clarity. |
| equally as good as | Say "as good as" or "equally good." |
| etc. etc. | One "etc." is usually sufficient. |
| ever...yet | Do not say, "No one has ever undersold us **yet**." |
| far **more** worse | Do not say, "Business is far **more** worse this year than last." Say "far worse" or "much worse." |
| finish **off** | "Off is frequently used but unnecessary, as in "Finish **off** that correspondence before you leave." |
| first before | Should only be used for emphasis, as in "Investigate first; invest later." |
| first begin | Use for exactness, as in "When they first begin the job, make sure they have the proper tools." |
| follows after | "Follows" implies "after." May be used for special emphasis. |
| **free** gratis | "Gratis" means "free." |
| help **from** | Do not say, "She couldn't help **from** crying when she saw what had happened." |
| in among<br>in around<br>in back of<br>in between<br>in under | These are usually careless constructions. On occasion they are justified as in "It was slipped in among the order forms on his desk." |
| inside **of** | Say "inside the office building" rather than "inside **of** the office building." |
| joint partnership | "Partnership often implies "joint ownership," but not always. There are several kinds of partnership; but only use the word "joint" when it is absolutely necessary for clarity. |
| like **for** | Do not say, "We would like **for** you to join us at dinner." |

*Appendix IX–Superfluous Words*

| | |
|---|---|
| near **to** | Do not say, "near **to** our plant." |
| **new** beginner | The only time you might want to use the word "new" here is when there are several beginners and a new one arrives. |
| not **a** one | Use "not one." |
| Off **of** or off **from** | Do not say, "She fell off **of** the forklift." |
| **often** accustomed to<br>**often** in the habit of | It is incorrect to say, "He was **often** accustomed to being blamed for delays." |
| old adage | An "adage" is old by definition; hence this expression is redundant. But it is so common that some experts consider it acceptable. |
| outside **of** | It is better to say "outside our property" rather than "outside **of** our property." |
| over **with** | Do not say, "He was glad the meeting was over **with**." |
| pretend **like** | Do not say, "They pretend **like** they don't know what we're talking about." |
| remember **of** | Do not say, "He didn't remember **of** our phone conversation" or "Not that I remember **of**." |
| repeat **again** | The only time this would be acceptable is when a thing has already been repeated once; then it can be repeated again. |
| revert **back** | Redundant. "Revert" by definition means "to go back." |
| **same** identical | Redundant. Never say, "We offered her the same identical salary she received before." Use one word or the other. |
| such as,<br>**for example**<br>as, **for instance** | Use one or the other, but not both |
| think **for** | Do not say, "More than we think **for**." |
| those **ones** | Do not say, "When you clean up the used boxes, don't forget those **ones** in the corner." |
| **up** above | Do not say, "I think I left it **up** above the stack of index cards on the shelf." |
| **up** until | "Until" means "up to the time of." Do not say, "We'll give him **up** until Friday to come up with the cash." |

NOTE—In some cases, it is acceptable to indulge in a certain amount of redundancy. Review the list of well-known phrases below which may appear to contain redundancies but are actually slightly different in meaning:

    due and payable

    over and above

    save and except

    one and the same thing

    good and sufficient reasons

    each and every

    unless and until

    right, title, or interest.

# Appendix X

# The Right Preposition

One of the most common errors in writing involves the use of prepositions in certain phrases. The wrong preposition can completely change your intended meaning. Unfortunately, there is no set rule for the combining of prepositions with other words. Some combinations are established idioms and are used because they "sound right." Others are determined by their meanings. The list below includes examples of both.

| | |
|---|---|
| abashed at/before/in | She felt abashed at her actions<br>The prisoner was abashed before the judge.<br>The thief was abashed in the presence of the jury. |
| abounds in/with | The country abounds in uranium deposits.<br>The river abounds with fish. |
| abhorrence of | We expressed our abhorrence of his actions. |
| absolve from | She was absolved from blame in the incident. |
| accompanied by/with | They were accompanied by a police officer.<br>His offer was accompanied with a smile. |
| acquiesce in | We had no choice but to acquiesce in the matter. |
| acquit of/with | He was acquitted of the crime in 1973.<br>She acquitted herself with credit. |
| adapted to/for/from | She adapted to her new environment quickly.<br>The car had been adapted for carrying dogs.<br>The design of the dress was adapted from that of a man's suit. |
| admit of/to | The situation admits of no compromise.<br>We shall never be admitted to her confidence. |
| agreeable to | If you're agreeable to our plans, give us a call. |
| alien to | Forcing the issue was alien to her personality. |
| allegiance from/to | The government exacts allegiance from the citizens.<br>She showed her allegiance to her employer. |
| alongside | (preposition "of" is considered unnecessary)<br>He ran alongside the car. |

| | |
|---|---|
| analogous to | This role in the play is analogous to the part of the mother in the other play. |
| angry at/with/about | I'm angry at the way things were handled.<br>I'm angry with John for not showing up.<br>I'm angry about the election. |
| approve of | I don't approve of the way she dresses. |
| apropos of | (or no preposition) Her comment was apropos of nothing. |
| assist in/at/with | She assisted in cleaning the house.<br>She assisted at the party.<br>She assisted with the funeral arrangements. |
| astonished at/by | I was astonished at her childish behavior.<br>We were astonished by her maturity. |
| attest to | Your scores attest to how hard you've worked this semester. |
| aversion to | I have a real aversion to meat. |
| beneficial to | Proper eating habits are beneficial to your health. |
| break with/from/in | His decision represented a break with tradition.<br>She tried to break away from her parents by moving to the city.<br>The two countries suffered a break in diplomatic relations. |
| cause of/for | The broken pump was the cause of the flooding.<br>The sunshine was cause for celebration. |
| choose among/between | He had to choose between the two equally well qualified candidates.<br>She had to choose among several inviting possibilities. |
| compare to/with | I compared the house to a shoebox.<br>Compared with last year, our profits this year are minimal. |
| compatible with | Any dry white wine would be compatible with this meal. |
| complementary to | Their findings were complementary to our own. |
| compliance with | In compliance with the law, we paid our tax bill on time. |
| conceive of | I can't conceive of their getting married in the near future. |
| concur in/with | The rest of the board members concurred in the decision.<br>We concurred with his parents and sent him home early. |
| conducive to | Wet soil is more conducive to growing some types of plants than others. |
| confide in/to | She confided in me before she left.<br>He confided his personal papers to me before he left. |
| conform to/<br>in conformity with | Her appearance conformed to the dress code.<br>In conformity with the dress code, she never wore slacks. |
| consist in/of | Understanding consists in maintaining an open mind.<br>The paste consisted of flour and water. |
| consistent in/with | He was not consistent in his arguments.<br>Her statements were not consistent with her feelings. |
| contemporary with | He was contemporary with Proust, but not nearly as well known. |
| contrast with | (when contrast is a verb) It was difficult not to contrast her with her peers. |

*Appendix X–The Right Preposition*

| | |
|---|---|
| contrast to/with | (when contrast is a noun) She presented quite a contrast to her environment.<br>In contrast with her surroundings, she looked like a queen. |
| correspond to/with | The plans don't correspond to the architect's design.<br>I correspond with my parents regularly. |
| credit for | He got the credit for the program's success. |
| cure of | The medication failed to cure her of the disease. |
| danger in/of | There is danger in acting precipitously.<br>There is always a danger of capsizing when you canoe in the spring. |
| die by/from/of | He died by drowning.<br>He died from suffocation.<br>He died of grief.<br>(Note: Use "by" when you mean "to die by the process of"; use "from" when you mean "to die from the effects of an outside agent"; use "of" when you mean "to die from the effects of an internal agent.") |
| differ from/with | I differ from my mother in temperament.<br>I differ with you on that point. |
| different from/than | "Different from" is the preferred usage here, although "different than" is widely used. |
| disappointed in/with | She was disappointed in her son's performance.<br>She was disappointed with the the recipe's results. |
| discourage from | I hate to discourage you from attending, but you'll thank me later. |
| disgusted by/with | I am disgusted by her behavior.<br>I am disgusted with her. |
| dispense with | I think we can dispense with the explanation. |
| dissent from | They expressed their dissent from the committee's stand without hesitation. |
| dissociate from | All he wanted was to dissociate himself from the whole situation. |
| enamored of/with | I'm so enamored of her.<br>I am enamored with the view from the tower. |
| foreign to | Anger was totally foreign to her personality and upbringing. |
| free from/of | The population is almost entirely free from hunger.<br>I'm glad to be free of her. |
| identical with/to | Their proposals were identical with the guidelines.<br>My situation is identical to yours. |
| ill with | She was ill with the flu. |
| immune to | He was immune to her charms. |
| incompatible with | The board's attitudes were incompatible with our own. |
| incongruous with | The pink wallpaper was incongruous with the expensive paintings in the room. |
| incorporate in/into/with | The provision was incorporated in the constitution.<br>The new cabinets were incorporated into the plans for the kitchen.<br>The new company was incorporated with the existing three firms. |
| independent of | The child's behavior showed how independent of her mother she had become. |

| | |
|---|---|
| indifferent to | I was completely indifferent to their complaints. |
| inseparable from | One twin was inseparable from the other. |
| insight into | The lecture gave us valuable insight into the author's work. |
| intercede for/with | You should intercede for her, even if she's guilty.<br>Intercede with the judge if you can. |
| intent on/upon | I was intent on winning the game.<br>I was so intent upon winning that I lost sight of my opponent's moves. |
| jealous of/for | He was jealous of me.<br><br>I was jealous for her sake. |
| justified in | I think he was entirely justified in refusing to attend the meeting. |
| labor at/for/under | She labored all night at her sewing.<br>She labored ceaselessly for the cause.<br>She labored under the same boss for 15 years. |
| level at/to/with | Don't level that gun at me.<br>The historic structure was leveled to the ground.<br>The shelf is level with the top of the table. |
| martyr for/to | He was a martyr for his party's beliefs.<br>He was a martyr to the disease. |
| monopoly of | The telephone company had a monopoly of the area.<br>(could also be "monopoly on") |
| motive for | She had no motive for being so cruel. |
| necessity for/of/to | I saw the necessity for decisive action.<br>I realize the necessity of acting swiftly.<br>Your support is a necessity to me. |
| need for/of | The need for medical treatment is obvious.<br>The house was in need of a fresh coat of paint. |
| oblivious of/to | He was oblivious of his obligations.<br>(meaning "forgetful of")<br>He was oblivious to her tears." (meaning "aloof toward") |
| occasion of/for | Her outspokenness was the occasion of much discomfort.<br>You had no occasion for being so outspoken. |
| occupied by/with | The room was occupied by mourners dressed in black.<br>They were occupied with their work. |
| opposite to/of | The house was opposite to the run-down factory.<br>("to" is often dropped)<br>Her appearance was the opposite of well-groomed. |
| opposition to | One group was in opposition to the other. |
| parallel to/with | The course ran parallel to the river.<br>We were unable to parallel our progress with that of our competitors. |
| part from/with | It was so difficult to part from the child.<br>It was difficult to part with our possessions. |
| payment for/of | He had barely enough to make his monthly payment for the groceries.<br>His payment of the fee was three weeks late. |
| permission from/of | I received permission from the lawyers to make a public statement.<br>With the permission of the lawyers, I made a public statement. |

## Appendix X – The Right Preposition

| | |
|---|---|
| persevere in/against | He persevered in his devotion to running until he was well into his seventies.<br>He persevered against all opposition. |
| prerequisite of/to | Two math courses are a prerequisite of graduation.<br>Baptism is prerequisite to acceptance into the church. |
| prevail against/upon | The will to live often prevails against terminal illness.<br>She prevailed upon us to help her. |
| prohibit from | We were prohibited from participating in the demonstration. |
| purpose in/of | His purpose in leaving was unknown.<br>The purpose of his decision was to make us angry. |
| reconcile to/with | She was reconciled to living her life alone.<br>She was unable to reconcile her beliefs with her employer's demands. |
| recover from | It took him over a year to recover from the financial setback. |
| resentment toward/at | She bore no resentment toward us for winning the argument.<br>Her resentment at the insult was justified. |
| rests in/on/with | The success of the firm rests in its commitment to service.<br>Their failure to reach a decision rests on the continuing conflict between the chairman and the board members.<br>That responsibility rests with the President. |
| revenge for/upon | He wanted revenge for the way he'd been treated.<br>He took his revenge upon the individuals responsible for hurting him. |
| sanction of/for | He had the sanction of the law to back him up.<br>The committee gave him their sanction for whatever course of action he chose to take. |
| sick with | She was home sick with a cold. |
| similarity to/of | The family members show little similarity to each other.<br>The similarity of the brothers is marked. |
| stock in/of | I don't take much stock in his argument.<br>Take stock of the alternatives before you make your decision. |
| subscribe for/to | We subscribed for the purpose of demonstrating where we stood on the issue.<br>We subscribed to the newspaper. |
| suffer from/with | I suffer from asthma.<br>We had no choice but to suffer with him for the time being. |
| suitable to/for | His behavior was more suitable to the courtroom than the living room.<br>The dress was perfectly suitable for a wedding. |
| superior to | This investment is far superior to the other alternatives we've explored. |
| surround by/with | The village was surrounded by water.<br>The only way to win the battle was to surround the village with troops and cut off the supply lines. |
| sympathy in/for/with | We have sympathy in your sorrow.<br>We have sympathy for your uncle.<br>I have sympathy with his ambitions. |
| vary from/with | This portrait varies from the earlier one in several respects.<br>Each of the group members varied with the others, and no significant decisions were reached. |

| | |
|---|---|
| vulnerable to | Her wealth made her vulnerable to many unscrupulous suitors. |
| wait for/on | I've been waiting for something good to happen to her.<br>Don't wait on me — I'll serve myself. |
| withheld from | The money was withheld from her wages. |
| zeal in/for | He shows tremendous zeal in his work.<br>He has demonstrated his zeal for the nuclear freeze movement. |

# Appendix XI

# Commonly Misspelled Words

Nothing takes the professional touch out of your writing like a misspelled word. Notice how "right" most of the "wrong" words below appear at first glance:

| RIGHT | WRONG |
|---|---|
| absorbent | absorbant |
| absorption | absorbtion |
| accommodate | accomodate |
| achieve | acheive |
| acquiesce | aquiese |
| acquire | aquire |
| advise | advize |
| adolescence | adolesence |
| all right | alright |
| analysis | analisis |
| analyze | analize |
| apparent | apparant |
| appearance | appearence |
| arguing | argueing |
| assistance | assistence |
| athlete | athalete |
| attendance | attendence |
| banana | bannana |
| basically | basicly |
| beginner | beginer |
| belief | beleif |
| benefited | benefitted |
| brethren | bretheren |
| Britain | Britian |
| buoyancy | bouyancy |
| business | buisness |
| capital | capitle |

| RIGHT | WRONG |
|---|---|
| category | catagorey |
| chauffeur | chauffuer |
| chimneys | chimnies |
| clothes | cloths |
| coliseum | colosium |
| colossal | collosal |
| commitment | committment |
| committee | commitee |
| comparative | comparitive |
| concede | consede |
| conceive | concieve |
| conscientious | conscientous |
| consensus | concensus |
| controversial | controvercial |
| corrugated | corrigated |
| criticize (preferred) | criticise (British, allowed) |
| curriculum | curiculum |
| cynical | synical |
| deuce | duece |
| definite | defanite |
| dependent | dependant |
| develop | develope |
| disappoint | dissapoint |
| disastrous | disasterous |
| ecstasy | ecstacy |
| embarrass | embarass |
| equipped | equiped |
| exaggerate | exagerate |
| existence | existance |
| fallacy | fallasy |
| February | Febuary |
| fiery | firey |
| flammable | flamable |
| forty | fourty |
| friend | freind |
| fulfill | fullfill |
| gnawing | knawing |
| government | goverment |
| grammar | grammer |
| guarantee | gaurantee |
| guidance | guidence |
| height | heighth |
| hemorrhage | hemorrage |
| hindrance | hinderance |
| hygiene | hygeine |
| hypocrisy | hipocrisy |
| idiosyncrasy | idiosyncracy |
| incense | insense |
| incidentally | incidently |
| independent | independant |
| infallible | infalable |
| inoculate | innoculate |
| insistence | insistance |
| intercede | intersede |
| interfered | interferred |
| jeopardize | jeprodize |
| kimono | kimona |

| RIGHT | WRONG |
|---|---|
| laid | lade |
| leisure | liesure |
| license | lisense |
| lonely | lonley |
| maintenance | maintainance |
| management | managment |
| maneuver | manuveur |
| mischief | mischeif |
| mortgaged | morgaged |
| necessary | necessry |
| Negroes | Negros |
| nickel | nickle |
| ninety | ninty |
| noticeable | noticable |
| nowadays | nowdays |
| occasionally | ocassionaly |
| occurred | ocurred |
| occurrence | occurence |
| opponent | oponent |
| optimism | optomism |
| pamphlet | pamflet |
| parallel | parrallel |
| performance | performence |
| permissible | permissable |
| personal | personel |
| persuade | pursuade |
| plagiarism | plaigarism |
| possess | posess |
| precede | preceed |
| precipice | presipice |
| preferred | perferred |
| prevalent | prevelant |
| privilege | privelege |
| probably | probly |
| proceed | procede |
| propeller | propellor |
| psychological | psycological |
| publicly | publically |
| questionnaire | questionaire |
| realize | realise |
| recipient | resipient |
| recommend | reccomend |
| relevant | relevent |
| renown | reknown |
| repel | repell |
| repetition | repitition |
| rhapsody | rapsody |
| rhododendron | rhododrendon |
| rhubarb | ruhbarb |
| rhythm | rythm |
| sacrilegious | sacreligious |
| safety | saftey |
| scissors | sissors |
| seize | sieze |
| separate | seperate |

| RIGHT | WRONG |
|---|---|
| shepherd | sheperd |
| similar | similiar |
| sincerity | sincerety |
| sophomore | sophmore |
| subtle | sutle |
| suing | sueing |
| supersede | supercede |
| surreptitious | sureptitous |
| temperament | temperment |
| tragedy | tradgedy |
| transferable | transferrable |
| unparalleled | unparalelled |
| usage | useage |
| vaccine | vacine |
| vacuum | vaccuum |
| vegetable | vegtable |
| villain | villian |
| Wednesday | Wensday |
| weird | wierd |
| yield | yeild |

PN 1115 .B88 1986

| DATE DUE | | | |
|---|---|---|---|
| | | | |
| | | | |
| | | | |
| | | | |
| | | | |
| | | | |
| | | | |
| | | | |
| | | | |
| | | | |
| | | | |
| | | | |
| | | | |

PN 1115 .B88 1986